What Legal Professionals Are Saying About the Breaking Poverty Barriers to Equal Justice Training

We lawyers and judges are called upon not only to be competent legal technicians, but also to deeply understand, empathize with and provide trusted guidance. This training by Dr. Beegle is essential.

Judge Bruce Peterson
Minnesota Fourth Judicial District

This training will help lawyers get better outcomes for their clients across the country.

Judge Jay Quam
Minnesota Fourth Judicial District

Sometimes it's difficult for lawyers who have not lived in poverty.
Some of the best pieces of the training were the insights into the perspectives that people who live in poverty have.

David March
Senior Counsel, Target Corporation

A lot of what I'll take away is how I can better communicate with and understand my clients and what they're going through.

Mike Skoglund
Senior Counsel, Cargill, Inc.

It's helpful for me to think of where our pro bono attorneys are at, whether they've been exposed to this kind of training before and making sure our clients and attorneys are prepared for each other.

Anne Applebaum
Pro Bono Director
Immigrant Law Center of Minnesota

Breaking Poverty Barriers to Equal Justice

COMPANION GUIDEBOOK TO THE VIDEO TRAINING:

BREAKING POVERTY BARRIERS TO EQUAL JUSTICE

Dr. Donna M. Beegle

Breaking Poverty Barriers to Equal Justice
Companion Guidebook to the Video Training: Breaking Poverty Barriers
to Equal Justice
Dr. Donna M. Beegle

By: Dr. Donna Beegle
Editors: Debbie Ellis, Martha Delaney, and Cory Jubitz
Design and layout by Deborah Perdue of Illumination Graphics,
illuminationgraphics.com

Communication Across Barriers • www.combarriers.com
(503) 590-4599 • PO Box 23071, Tigard, OR 97281-3071

Additional copies of this book and DVD are available for purchase.
For details, email books@combarriers.com
or visit www.storecombarriers.com

Published in the United States of America by Communication Across
Barriers, Inc., PO Box 23071, Tigard, OR 97281

The Breaking Barriers to Equal Justice project is the culmination of many years of work with low income individuals seeking legal assistance and is the result of a dedicated group of partners with the passion and vision to help break the cycle of poverty and increase equal access to justice.

ABOUT THE TRAINING

The Breaking Poverty Barriers to Equal Justice training is specifically designed to assist legal professionals in improving access to justice. The training aims to improve attorney-client relationships and communication. The goals are better outcomes for clients and greater satisfaction for legal professionals like you.

These materials offer education enabling you to recognize, understand, and transcend the poverty barriers that prevent equal justice. This curriculum provides a lens on poverty in general, how the conditions of poverty erect barriers to accessing our legal system, and how legal professionals can work to improve access to justice for those in poverty. It explains how those in poverty experience our society and our court system. It provides concrete tools to better understand and represent clients from poverty.

Because of this training, you will:

1. Understand why more information about poverty is essential for breaking equal-justice barriers.

2. Better understand how people living in the crisis of poverty experience the legal system.

3. Develop skills for identifying and overcoming unconscious bias that can get in the way of serving people living in poverty.

4. Gain tools for effectively communicating and relating with clients in poverty.

5. Describe five keys for breaking poverty barriers to equal justice and provide examples of how you can implement them in your work with clients who live in poverty.

More specific learning objectives are provided at the beginning of each of the five modules.

USING THIS GUIDEBOOK

If you are doing this training on your own, this reference guide serves as a summary of the concepts covered in the Breaking Poverty Barriers to Equal Justice video training. This guidebook challenges you to reflect deeply on what you believe about poverty and the clients you serve who are living in the crisis of poverty. Please use the lessons learned to explore where you gained your ideas about poverty and how your perspectives impact how you communicate with and relate to those you serve. This guidebook also provides you with strategies and action steps for improving outcomes. (For more in-depth learning on poverty, please refer to the book *"See Poverty . . . Be the Difference."*)

The modules in this guidebook correlate with the video, allowing you to use it in a number of ways:

- Preview the Breaking Poverty Barriers to Equal Justice guidebook to familiarize yourself with the course content before watching the video.

- . Use your notes from the guidebook to promote discussion and action among co-workers, clients, and judges.

- Examine the Case Study as it unfolds throughout the module and use its story to help apply the learning to your own work. The case studies are based on true stories. They are not the depiction of one person, but a compilation of a few individuals to add depth to the story and portray the complexity of the nature of poverty within the legal system. All names have been changed to provide anonymity.

- Explore the "Extra!" activity pages and perform the exercises provided, before or after watching the video, to enhance your learning and implementation of the concepts. These "Extra!" activities are designed to allow for further learning and understanding of how to break poverty barriers to equal justice. These "Extra!" activities include new concepts, along with opportunities to apply the core ideas.

Each module is topic-specific, and each features key concepts, suggestions for what you can do, and additional content not covered in the video segments.

FACILITATING A TRAINING

If you are facilitating a training for a group of people, we recommend:
- Starting with an introduction of yourself and what draws you to this work.

- Giving attendees the context of the failure of our legal system to work for those in poverty (you can use Justice Lillehaug's remarks as a guide, if you wish).

- Giving participants five minutes prior to doing each module to answer the corresponding reflection questions (information about which will be presented in the video).

- Facilitating discussion around the question or exercise when the video stops for an exercise.

This entire program is estimated to last 4.5 hours. If you wish to shorten the presentation, you can cover some sections as a group and introduce participants to some materials to complete later on their own time.

In Appendix B is a sample description of the training in the event you wish to apply for CLE credit. (This one was tailored for Minnesota and for the special category of Elimination of Bias credit.)

ABOUT THE VIDEO

The video training, Breaking Poverty Barriers to Equal Justice, contains an introduction followed by five learning modules. It is recommended that participants watch the modules in order, as content is introduced and built upon as the modules progress. The length of each section is as follows:

Section	Approximate Length
Introduction	3 minutes
Module 1	21 minutes
Module 2	49 minutes
Module 3	14 minutes
Module 4	28 minutes
Module 5	14 minutes

Legal Beegle

At various points in the video, Legal Beegle activities will appear on the screen. These Legal Beegle activities are opportunities for you to better understand the concepts and to personalize the learning for a lasting impact. When you see a Legal Beegle activity slide, this is your cue to stop the video and proceed with the activity. When you complete the activity, resume the video.

NEED FOR THE TRAINING – THE CHALLENGE WE FACE

Per the Model Rules of Professional Responsibility, all lawyers are required *to explain a matter to the extent reasonably necessary to permit a client to make informed decisions regarding representation and to devote professional time and resources and use civic influence to ensure equal access to our system of justice for all those who because of economic or social barriers cannot afford or secure adequate legal counsel.* We have a responsibility not only to provide representation to those in poverty, but to contribute to efforts to make our system of justice work for all in our community, to understand and find ways to break these poverty and other barriers, and to ensure all in our communities receive the legal protections necessary for stability and well-being.

One huge barrier to our country realizing its vision of equal justice for all is recognizing that many of those who provide access to legal services are used to communicating and processing information in ways that are not accessible or familiar to people living in the crisis of poverty. As a result, not only does the message sent not equal the message received, we are often unaware that miscommunication and misunderstandings have occurred.

Without communication that leads to shared understanding, we are failing *"to explain a matter to the extent reasonably necessary to permit a client to make informed decisions regarding representation."* Our advice and legal services can then miss the mark for what the client really needs, leaving so many in our communities without meaningful access to legal protections.

Adding to these challenges is the equally invisible challenge of understanding the experiences that clients living in poverty face on a daily basis. It is human to use our own experiences as points of references for understanding and we can fall into assuming that our clients could/should "do what we would do." If they make a decision we don't understand, we may assume they are "irresponsible." If they don't follow a "simple" instruction, we may assume they "don't care." Without understanding the context of their lives, we can miss that, what may not take much effort for us, such as gathering paperwork, can be prohibitively time consuming and confusing for people desperately juggling numerous crises or demands on their time. What may be obvious or doable for a legal professional may be next to impossible for someone facing the crisis of poverty.

It's not that legal professionals are not trying. So many of us represent clients on a pro bono basis and make tremendous efforts to bring them the law's protections. If a client is late, we may shoulder on with the meeting, despite what feels like disrespect to our time. This feeling of disrespect can and does impact our communication and behavior toward our client, whether we are aware of it or not. If the client does not return phone calls, we redouble our efforts by calling and texting more. When the client doesn't bring the paperwork, we repeat the reason for the paperwork and send them away to try again. We find ourselves wondering why we are working so hard when it appears to us that the client isn't. And, if we altogether lose touch with a client, our beliefs about poverty – often based on the media – are confirmed. If people in poverty would only apply themselves, they could avoid half of their troubles.

There is a way out of this trap, and it involves working smarter, not harder. This training provides us with the steps and strategies for doing do this, including showing us:

- Some contexts of poverty – to assist us in understanding the lives and challenges of people in different contexts of poverty so we can meet people where they are and to set them up for successful outcomes.

- How to avoid the most common destroyer of effective communication – judgment of others.

- Why our clients from poverty may feel betrayed by the legal system in general and the importance of and suggestions for establishing trust.

- Two fundamental ways of communicating (print and oral communication styles) and strategies for ensuring we understand our client's histories and priorities and they understand our explanations and advice.

- Five ways to reframe the problem of equal justice – so we have more proven strategies for making justice more accessible to more individuals in our communities.

As in all situations requiring adaptive change, reducing barriers to equal justice for all will not be solved by doing the same things with more energy, but by consciously changing our perspective of the problem. Gaining poverty competency may initially require extra time and effort, but in the long run, it will increase our effectiveness for our clients in poverty, increase our professional satisfaction, and ultimately contribute to efforts in our community that undermine the conditions leading to poverty. And it is the only way we will meet our professional obligation to promote equal justice for all in our communities.

TABLE OF CONTENTS

1) Strengths
2) Resiliency
3) Asset
4) Faulty Attrib.
5) Social Capital
   — mentoring

Activity: Practical thing
Share Mine

LIST OF ACTIVITIES

INTRODUCTION
A MESSAGE FROM JUSTICE DAVID LILLEHAUG, MINNESOTA SUPREME COURT

For too many people, our legal system is not working the way it should. People living in poverty, especially, lack the legal representation they need to achieve fair and impartial results.

People in poverty face any number of daily crises, ranging from unpredictable childcare, to starting an unreliable car, to deciding whether to pay the electric bill or buy food. It can be absolutely overwhelming if, on top of all of these "no-win" situations, one also encounters a legal crisis: a landlord/tenant conflict, a custody issue, a debt buyer pursuing a lien, an immigration problem, or the need for a criminal expungement just to apply for a job.

The legal profession has a long history of free or low-cost legal services. But many of us are not well-equipped to do this work. We need to improve our understanding of poverty and its profound impact on clients' lives so we can serve them more effectively.

It's a sad fact that too many attorney-client relationships break down because of miscommunication and incorrect assumptions. In as many as 25 percent of cases in which a person in poverty has a lawyer, either the attorney or client ends up withdrawing. The prejudice to all is incalculable.

That's why the Breaking Poverty Barriers to Equal Justice training presented here is so important. And that's why I was so pleased to participate in it. The goals of the Breaking Poverty Barriers to Equal Justice curriculum are better outcomes for clients and greater satisfaction for legal professionals. The guidebook and video provide practical tools and strategies for attorneys to improve services and promote equal justice for those living in poverty.

Dr. Donna Beegle, who will take you through the training, grew up in generational poverty. She explains the existence of different kinds of poverty, including generational, situational, and immigrant. Within five minutes, you'll see that she's completely authentic as she explains how those in poverty tend to view authority figures. You'll learn, for example, how the survival and communication skills of poverty clash with the traditional rules and culture of our justice system. You'll learn why someone raised in generational poverty experiences shame, distrust and fear of outsiders—including you, their attorney. And you'll learn why you and your new client may have difficulty working together, whether it's scheduling appointments or communicating by email.

By the end of this training, you'll be in a position to better relate to, communicate with, and assist the people who most need your legal help. You'll improve your pro bono practice, better fulfill your professional responsibilities, and maybe—just maybe—even enhance the legal work for which you get paid!

Thanks for taking the time to participate in this important training!

INTRODUCTION FROM DR. BEEGLE

"My poverty experiences taught me that no one cares about people in poverty. What I realized when I was getting my education was that it wasn't that legal professionals and others who were making it did not care. It was that they did not know the poverty conditions we were experiencing. They could not know my daily life experience of generational poverty any more than I could understand their middle-class experiences."

—Donna Beegle

Thank you so much for being willing to go on this learning journey with me! My work and my passions are all about making a difference for people who live in the crisis of poverty. I appreciate your willingness to gain knowledge, explore strategies, and add your wisdom to these materials. My hope is that together we can make our legal system work better for those living in the crisis of poverty.

Our legal system is built upon the assumption that all who participate in it will have the help of a lawyer. However, at least 75 percent of the time, people living in the crisis of poverty cannot find a lawyer to help them with critical issues related to family, housing, criminal expungement, employment, and taxes. Providing low-cost/pro-bono service as an attorney is one way to solve this problem, yet the challenges to improving legal services go beyond this alone. It also requires improving the provision of services.

Without a lawyer, whether or not they ever appear in a courtroom, people in poverty forgo accurate knowledge of their rights and a powerful negotiator and problem-solver in their corner. When they do go to court alone, without the knowledge of the rules of civil procedure by which all judges are bound, they are much less likely to receive favorable results. Judges try to make fair decisions but simply may not have all the facts or arguments they need.

Unfortunately, for those in generational poverty, simply getting an attorney does not guarantee access to legal services or the law's protections.

As a legal professional, you have a unique power to break these poverty barriers and ensure *all* in our communities receive the legal protections they need for stability and well-being—by learning and building upon these 10 foundational skill sets:

1. Understanding how we arrived at our current ideas about poverty and the people who live in it.

2. Knowing the facts and structural causes of poverty to ensure that you are not holding subconscious bias and operating on stereotypes.

3. Understanding the complexities of poverty and how many different life experiences are labeled "poverty."

4. Operating on the assumption that people in poverty are making the best decisions they can in the "shoes" they are wearing.

5. Creating relationships built on shared understandings that support trust.

6. Fostering a welcoming climate where everyone belongs and has knowledge to contribute.

7. Developing and implementing policies and services that take into consideration the life experiences of clients living in poverty.

8. Honoring oral-culture styles of communicating and relating.

9. Helping clients navigate the court system's print culture to ensure clients understand the words/examples that are being used.

10. Building your networks so that you have a "resource backpack" to share with clients that will lesson, and, in some cases, eradicate the impacts of poverty.

With these competencies, you will better comprehend and overcome the barriers that prevent your clients in poverty from fully participating in the legal system. When representing a client from poverty, you will be more able to ensure that your hard work makes a difference in his or her life.

It is nearly impossible to overstate the power legal professionals like you have to make a difference in our communities. Our legal system has been failing to serve up to a quarter of those in our communities…but you hold in your hands an important key for improving legal outcomes for people living in the crisis of poverty. I am excited to engage in this journey with you and look forward to hearing about the difference *you* make in your clients' lives and in the legal system.

LEGAL BEEGLE ACTIVITY

Legal Beegle

Test Your Knowledge of the Impacts of Poverty on Legal Services

Please circle true (T) or false (F). Answers found in Appendix A, page 118.

1. For every person served by a Legal Services Corporation–funded program, one person who seeks help is turned down because of insufficient resources.　**T or F**

2. Three out of five people in poverty who apply for legal services have the assistance of either a private attorney (pro bono or paid) or a legal aid lawyer.　**T or F**

3. A family of four with an annual income of $35,000 or less qualifies for legal services.　**T or F**

4. Nationally, only one legal aid attorney is available for every 6,415 low-income people.　**T or F**

5. Studies show that the vast majority of people who appear without representation do so because they are unable to afford it.　**T or F**

6. People who represent themselves have outcomes similar to those who have legal representation.　**T or F**

7. The Legal Services Corporation defines the "justice gap" as when people in poverty are not getting legal services for criminal defense.　**T or F**

8. There continues to be a major gap between the civil legal needs of low-income people and the legal help that they receive.　**T or F**

9. The majority of people in poverty receiving legal assistance are men.　**T or F**

10. A District of Columbia legal needs study reported that 98 percent of both petitioners and respondents in the Domestic Violence Unit of the D.C. Superior Court were represented; approximately 77 percent of plaintiffs involved in family law cases were represented; more than 98 percent of respondents involved in paternity and child support cases were represented; and 97 percent of respondents in fair housing or eviction cases were represented　**T or F**

SELF-REFLECTION:
How Might Your Experiences of the Court System Be Different from Those of Someone Living in Poverty?

What are *your* personal experiences of the justice system?

Please check all that apply.

☐ Parking ticket

☐ Traffic ticket

☐ Speeding ticket

☐ Loitering

☐ Panhandling

☐ Eviction

☐ Garnishment (wage or bank)

☐ Family court (divorce, custody)

☐ Juvenile court (child in need of protective services or termination of parental rights)

☐ Criminal court—misdemeanor (such as petty theft, possession, DUI/DWI, etc.)

☐ Criminal court—felony (such as burglary, shoplifting, arson, sex offense, etc.)

SELF-REFLECTION (cont.):
Have you ever broken the law? Were you caught? Have you ever been given the benefit of the doubt because you acted in ways that the decision-makers found respectable and credible? What language did you know that helped you operate in the system?

Write Your Thoughts Below

_____

_____

_____

_____

_____

_____

_____

_____

_____

_____

CASE STUDY!

YOUR FIRST MEETING WITH CHAD

You have accepted a pro bono custody case to help a single father regain visitation rights with his 6-year-old daughter, Whitney. All you know about the case is that the dad, Chad, is 41 years old. A few years ago, he lost physical custody of his daughter to his daughter's mother, Jamie. Now, Chad would like to have custody, joint custody, or—at the least—better court-ordered visitation so that he could see his daughter on a more regular basis.

Chad was a "no-show" for your first scheduled appointment. He called several days after the missed appointment—clearly stressed, but with no explanation of why he had missed his appointment. He requested a new appointment to review his case. Although you had second thoughts about setting another appointment with Chad, you made a second appointment with him and let him know that you only had 30 minutes on that day before you had to be in another meeting.

Today is his second scheduled appointment. It is already 10 minutes past his appointment. Once again, you have not heard from him. You don't know whether he is going to show up or not. A couple of minutes later, your secretary calls and lets you know that Chad is in the reception area.

You go out to the lobby to greet Chad. You are surprised by the person you meet in the waiting area. Chad is really thin and frail looking. He is about 5 feet 10 inches tall and can't weigh more than 110 pounds. His skin looks really thin and he has dark circles under his eyes. His hair is shaved close to his scalp. His clothes, although clean, are clearly too large for his small frame. He smells of marijuana. His attitude, instead of being one of apology, seems to be more of frustration and annoyance.

You invite him back to your office. He does not have any of the paperwork you had asked him to bring: He has no birth certificate or records for Whitney and no proof of residence. When asked about the issues that brought him to your office, he often repeats what you asked and provides only partial answers. He seems distracted. Because you had less than 12 minutes to chat with him, you feel really rushed and don't feel fully prepared to represent him. You ask him to come back in a couple of days with the required paperwork and ask him to fill out a client intake form for you.

Discussion/Reflection Questions

1. What was your first impression of Chad? What is your opinion of him?

2. Why do you assume Chad missed his first appointment and was late to his second?

3. Why do you think Chad does not have his paperwork in order?

4. Based on your interactions with Chad, how do you plan to represent him?

5. What questions do you need answered to effectively represent Chad?

MODULE 1

UNDERSTANDING POVERTY FROM AN INSIDER'S PERSPECTIVE: WHY IT'S ESSENTIAL TO BREAKING POVERTY BARRIERS TO EQUAL JUSTICE

Learning Objectives:

- Gain insights into how people living in poverty experience the justice system.

- Share why it is important for legal professionals to understand the experiences of those living in the crisis of poverty.

- Understand how vocabulary and different styles of communication can be barriers to accessing the legal system.

- Name where most people get their knowledge of what it's like to live in poverty.

- Identify some specific poverty barriers to obtaining equal justice.

- See why those in poverty may not even seek the assistance of a lawyer, and learn ways to remedy that.

- Know how the isolation of people living in poverty reduces access to justice.

- Describe the importance of legal professionals gaining self-awareness and self-reflection on their beliefs about poverty and those who live in it.

Video Length: 21 Minutes

THE IMPORTANCE OF AN INSIDER'S PERSPECTIVE

The majority of research and writing about poverty is done by people who have not experienced poverty. In this section, I will share some of my own experiences in generational poverty to give you a better sense of the chronic crises that some of your clients live with daily. I will give you an insider's perspective on what it is like to survive without a home, education, or skills to earn a living wage in a country that is known for its wealth and opportunities.

While my generational poverty experiences are not representative of all poverty experiences, my research and work have shown that the practices used to break barriers for people in generational poverty are also effective for people from working-class, immigrant, and situational poverty. On the contrary, strategies used to break poverty barriers based on race and/or situational poverty often fall short of addressing generational and working-class poverty barriers.

I use my personal story and research to illuminate a serious problem that perpetuates poverty: Professionals graduate from college without ever having had Poverty 101. These professionals go on to teach, counsel, serve, and make policy and funding decisions that often do not meet the needs of students and families living in the crisis of poverty. In fact, many of these policies and actions can inadvertently punish people in poverty conditions.

Without a grounded understanding of poverty, its history, and its impact on human beings, well-meaning professionals may miss opportunities to improve educational and life outcomes. Yet learning about different types of poverty experiences and poverty history is not enough to create meaningful change. In the case of the legal field, that learning needs to be put into action to improve attorney–client communication and trust.

The Present Justice Situation

- We have a justice system that works well for those who can afford representation and a very different justice system for those who cannot.

- Nationally, only one legal aid attorney is available for every 6,415 low-income people.

- Courts are facing significantly increased numbers of unrepresented litigants, who have worse outcomes than those who are represented.

www.combarriers.com

Communication
Across Barriers

Communication
Across Barriers

---

www.combarriers.com

The Present Situation

Communication
Across Barriers

Estimated time each legal aid attorney has to spend on a case...

- In New Orleans = 7 minutes
- In Detroit = 32 minutes
- In Atlanta = 39 minutes

Communication
Across Barriers

The Present Situation

A District of Columbia legal needs study reported:

•98% of petitioners and respondents in the Domestic Violence Unit of the D.C. Superior Court were unrepresented.

•77% of plaintiffs in family court were unrepresented.

•98% of respondents in paternity and child support cases were unrepresented.

•97% of respondents in fair housing and eviction court cases were unrepresented.

Communication
Across Barriers

Poverty Realities

- Life experiences teach that no one cares.

- You come to believe that everyone is smarter and better than you are.

- You do not feel like you belong in middle-class environments.

- Poverty teaches that education is not for you.

- There is no one to help.

Communication
Across Barriers

LEGAL BEEGLE ACTIVITY

Legal Beegle

Test Your Knowledge...of Poverty in America

Please respond true (T) or false (F) to the following statements.
Please answer all questions before checking answers. Answers
found in Appendix A, page 121.

1. Inequality of incomes has improved in the past 25 years. **T or F**

2. People graduate from colleges and universities to become doctors, lawyers, politicians, judges, social workers, educators and many other professions without ever having studied the history of poverty, its structural causes, or the models we have used to address poverty in America. **T or F**

3. People earning minimum wage are able to afford a modest two-bedroom apartment in America. **T or F**

4. The Federal Poverty Guidelines are an accurate indicator of how many people live in poverty in America. **T or F**

5. The majority of Americans believe poverty is caused by people's behavior and bad choices. **T or F**

6. Prison will solve poverty-related problems. **T or F**

7. People in poverty are to blame for drug and alcohol abuse, sex abuse, child abuse, domestic violence, and other social ills. **T or F**

8. Parents who do not go to school conferences do not care about their children. **T or F**

9. Head Start, the preschool program for children in poverty, is available to all 4-year-olds who live in poverty. **T or F**

10. People get rich by begging on the streets, getting welfare, and having babies to get more welfare. **T or F**

11. People in poverty are irresponsible because they buy cable television, cigarettes, and Nike shoes **T or F**

12. If you work hard, you will move up the economic ladder in the American labor market. **T or F**

THE DONNA BEEGLE STORY

I was born into a large, loving family! But, at an early age, I also learned that I had been born into the chaotic war zone of generational poverty. I soon felt the sting of the poverty "bullets" of hunger, untreated health issues, limited or inadequate access to transportation, constant evictions, being made fun of and not wanted, and never having enough money to make ends meet. I learned how these "bullets" would constantly knock us down and wound us physically, mentally, and emotionally.

Generational poverty means that your family often suffers because you have no money for health care or dental care. You never have a "personal physician" or annual check-ups to ensure that you are healthy. For generations, poor nutrition stole our health, energy and longevity. We mostly did without lunch unless we ate at school. Many nights, our dinner was just a spoonful of peanut butter or government cheese melted over tortilla chips. We rarely, if ever, ate vegetables.

Generational poverty also meant that, for many generations, most of my family members were illiterate. Because of our limited literacy, inadequate/incomplete education, and lack of specific job skills, we could not get jobs that would earn a living wage. My family members subsisted on temporary and seasonal work, migrant labor, and minimum-wage jobs—often requiring hard physical labor. While I was growing up, our family's biggest focus was making it through the day.

As with other families from generational poverty, my immediate family was highly mobile. We lived in multiple residences over my lifetime, including condemned rental houses, roach- and rat-infested motel rooms, trailers, storage units, and campgrounds. I can't remember a time when there weren't multiple generations and multiple extended family members living together under one small roof. Whenever necessary and possible, we slept in our cars or at relatives' homes. Sometimes, the river was our bath, while the gas station was our restroom.

My early experiences in impoverished schools shaped my views about myself and my expectations for the future—much like it did for my brothers. In school, I didn't understand what was going on. I didn't know the words my teachers used—as I was unable to understand and speak in their middle-class language. Every other sentence I spoke contained the word "ain't." I didn't know when it was proper to say "gone" or "went," "seen" or "saw." I didn't know the middle-class examples teachers used to explain the academic subjects. This just reinforced that there was something wrong with me and my family and friends. It reinforced that education was not for me. I internalized the poverty and its associated deficiencies to such a degree that I did not believe I was smart nor had anything to offer. I lost all hope and, like many people in generational poverty, I lived in survival mode.

Sex roles are more rigid in poverty. Like most males in poverty, the men in my family were socialized that they were "the protectors and providers" for their families. But, because they were born into poverty, they were not able to fulfill their societal role through obtaining a living-wage job. By around the age of 10, they started seeing the poverty and believing they needed to make it okay for the women in their lives. Sometimes, because their families are experiencing poverty, men are forced to leave their families in order for them to obtain services and get assistance. All my brothers did extraordinary things—all dropped out of school before graduating, one left the family, and others worked long, hard hours in unsafe jobs—to help the family survive.

My brothers also had to go outside the law—including sacrificing their reputations and giving up their freedom—to help the family survive. I can say I am the only member of my family who has not been incarcerated—not because I have never broken the law, but because I have been well protected by my loving brothers and allowed to fulfill my gender role of taking care of people rather than providing support for the family. My brothers have been jailed for minor offenses such as failure to pay child support, failure to pay fines for no car insurance, outstanding tickets, writing bad checks, and digging in dumpsters for cardboard/bottles for recycling. Others were jailed for longer periods of time for such offenses as burglary—stealing things to make life easier for the family or to use to sell to get money to pay the bills. I do not condone stealing. But, because of growing up in poverty, I learned to understand how and why it happens. My brothers were not genetically programmed to take the things our family needed or to break the law. The war zone of poverty taught those skills.

At 15 years old—after all the shame and humiliation at school—I dropped out of school to get married. When we married, my husband Jerry was 18 years old and had only a seventh-grade education from impoverished schools. He could read and write at about a second-grade level. We had our honeymoon in a cherry field in Wenatchee, Washington—meaning that after the ceremony we went to work picking cherries. Jerry and I soon began working full time for minimum wage at a foam rubber factory in Portland, Oregon. I had to lie about my age since it was illegal to hire a 15-year-old. Here, our adult lives became repeats of our childhoods. We worked hard but still had to make choices between rent and utilities. We continued to struggle with hunger, evictions, and not having our fundamental human needs met.

My dream—for as long as I could remember—was to be a mom. So, I got pregnant right after turning 17. During my pregnancy, I rarely saw a doctor and was not eligible for a medical card because Jerry was in the home and earning minimum wage at the foam rubber factory. My mom was my "doctor" and her education was from having six kids of her own. By the time I finally saw a doctor, he told me the baby was barely hanging in there. Joyce Marie was born almost three months early. She weighed 1 pound, 9 ounces, and was 8 1/2 inches long. She only lived for nine hours since her lungs were just too tiny to survive. I was devastated by her death.

My solution to the heartbreak of losing my daughter Joyce (and to fulfill my dream of being a mom) was to get pregnant as soon as possible. As with my first pregnancy, prenatal care and healthy foods were not part of my life. I was so afraid this baby would die just like Joyce Marie, but welfare policy would still not allow me to receive a medical card if Jerry was in the home. So, when I got afraid I would lose this baby, too, I lied to the welfare worker and said Jerry had left me. Because of that lie, I got a medical card in my fourth month of pregnancy. On March 23, 1979, Jennifer Marie was born two months prematurely. She was immediately put on a respirator and had an IV inserted into her stomach. When she was 11 days old, she underwent emergency heart surgery to close a hole in her heart. She had a 50 percent chance of surviving the surgery, and, if she lived, she would likely suffer from blindness and/or mental challenges. Jennifer survived the heart surgery and was kept on a respirator for two months. After two and a half months, when she finally weighed 5 pounds, I was able to take her home.

Since Jennifer was considered high risk, Oregon Health & Sciences University staff recommended that she receive priority placement for Head Start (HS), our nation's preschool program for children in poverty. The HS staff linked our family to the resources we desperately needed (e.g., the Women, Infants, and Children nutrition program, which provides juice, milk, and healthy foods to moms and their young children; temporary housing so we could move out of living in our car; etc.). I am convinced that it is due to these resources that I got to leave the hospital for the first time after three pregnancies with a healthy baby. Daniel weighed 6 pounds, 6 ounces.

During our marriage, Jerry and I subsisted on low-wage jobs—working in migrant labor, pizza parlors, retail, and manufacturing—or welfare. We moved from place to place, hoping for a better life. But we still could not earn enough to meet our basic needs. Just like we experienced growing up, we continued to have no health care. Our food was limited and our nutritional needs were not being met. The stress of poverty finally took a toll on our marriage. Jerry and I divorced after 10 years. By the age of 25, I was alone trying to care for my 6-year-old daughter (who was in the first grade) and 2-year-old son. But it wasn't long before we, too, were again evicted and homeless.

As a single mom, I applied for welfare. We were given $408 plus $150 in food stamps per month. With this, I found a place I could rent for $395 a month. Our house, located in a high-poverty/high-crime community, was broken into five times in a four-month period. With the remaining $13 after paying rent, I had to pay for utilities and transportation; buy clothing, soap, shampoo, toilet paper, and other basic necessities; and go to the laundromat. I was constantly making impossible choices—pay the rent or pay the bills, have my utilities shut off or get evicted.

After several months of juggling my payments like this, we were given an eviction notice and our lights were turned off for nonpayment. I went to a Community Action Agency to ask for help. The caseworker told me there was a new pilot welfare-to-work program, called Women in Transition (WIT), which was designed to be a three-week life skills program for displaced homemakers. Its goal was to help single women gain an education or skills to earn a living for their families.

At that point in my life, I had no hope or belief that a program could help me. I went to check it out—not thinking it would change anything, but not knowing what else to do. After the program director talked about the WIT program components, she informed us that we would be eligible for a Section 8 housing certificate if we completed the three-week life skills program. No one in my family of generations of homelessness had qualified for housing since we had never had the right address or right identification, or even knew how to fill out the paperwork for accessing housing support. Then and there I made up my mind—I would complete the program and secure housing so my babies would not be on the streets!

To my surprise, I completed the WIT program believing that I had something to offer. At last, I had hope. I wrote my dream in my diary: "I want to get a GED (general equivalency diploma) and maybe some-day take a journalism class. Then, I will be somebody and be able to take care of Jennifer and Daniel." This passionate motivation to take care of my two children remained constant throughout my educational journey. Supported with government resources to meet my family's basic needs, I was able to reach a milestone and obtain my GED at the age of 26.

Armed with hope, newfound confidence, and my WIT action plan, I went to my welfare worker and told her I wanted to pursue a two-year degree in journalism so I would not need government assistance any-more. She quickly told me that the state and federal welfare policies dictated that, in order to qualify for welfare, I needed to be available for any minimum-wage job. If I were in school, I would not be available, so the government would sanction me and cut my welfare check from $408 to $258 a month. I told the welfare worker, "Go ahead and cut my check if that's what you have to do. But I'm not going back to poverty. I'm going to college!"

At this time, the primary supports that kept me moving forward in the educational system were legal aid support that assisted me in having my housing needs met; the continued support of my family; and having mentors from the WIT program and Mt. Hood Community College/University of Portland who believed in me, encouraged me, and helped me navigate resources and opportunities to move forward while I journeyed the unknown path to higher education. Within 10 years, I earned an AA in journalism, a BA in communication, a master's degree in communication with a minor in gender studies, and a doctorate in educational leadership.

Today, I share my life experiences along with the insights I gained from years of studying poverty as I speak to and train educators, justice professionals, health care providers, social service providers, and other professionals across the nation who want to make a difference for those living in the crisis of poverty. For the past 25 years, I have traveled to hundreds of cities, covering 48 states and five countries to assist professionals with proven strategies for breaking poverty barriers.

Breaking Poverty Barriers to Equal Justice

www.combarriers.com

Communication
Across Barriers

- Understanding Poverty from an Insider's Perspective

- Defining Poverty and Understanding Its Impacts on Justice

- Examining Your Own Assumptions

- Improving Communication Across Poverty Barriers

- Five Keys to Better Serve Your Clients

Communication
Across Barriers

CASE STUDY!

CHAD'S LEGAL ISSUES— AN INSIDER PERSPECTIVE

For the third appointment, Chad arrives just a couple minutes after his scheduled start time. His hands are shaky and he looks as tired and stressed as at the last appointment. At least this time he brought some of the needed paperwork—a photocopy of Whitney's birth certificate and documentation from the place where he is living. But he neglected to fill out the client intake form.

From the paperwork and discussions, you learn that Chad is the father of two children: Mark, who is 14 years old, and Whitney, who is 6 years old. His two children are from two different mothers. Chad was never married to Mark's mother, Shannon. They had been neighborhood sweethearts since they were in middle school and had a long, on-again/off-again relationship because of Shannon's challenges with drugs. Even though they never had money for birth control, they didn't have a baby until Shannon got pregnant with Mark shortly after she turned 28 years old. Shannon continued her relationship with Chad after Mark's birth. When she would fall back into drug use, she would leave them for months at a time. Around the time Mark turned 3 years old, she finally decided that Mark was better off without her in his life—so she left Mark with Chad. She visited the two of them about once every year or so— whenever she felt she was clean and sober enough for a proper visit, but was unable to provide support of any kind. She was trapped in her drug addictions because she was unable to get the help she needed.

A few years later, Chad met Jamie at the minimum-wage job where they both worked. They soon married; and, a couple of years later, they had a beautiful baby girl they named Whitney. Even though they both were employed, they could not afford their own place, so they often struggled with homelessness. They were constantly moving—trying to find safe and stable housing. There was a lot of stress. Jamie finally convinced Chad to move to Phoenix, where her mother lived. A few days after they arrived, Jamie started a fight with Chad, and her mother called the police. Jamie told the police that Chad had attacked her, and her mother backed up her story. Chad was taken to jail, but the charges were dropped the following morning. He returned home and found that Jamie and her mom had put his things on the front lawn. He asked about his children. Jamie let him have Mark but told him that she and her mother were keeping Whitney. Desperate, Chad drove with Mark to the legal aid office. He had no savings and a limited income. Since his relatives were also in the crisis of poverty, they were unable to help him. He was put on a wait list for an attorney.

Chad tried every resource he could find to get an attorney to help him get joint custody of Whitney. After months of failed attempts to find legal help, he phoned a small law firm where an attorney agreed to take his case for the small payments he could make from his limited income. The attorney told Chad his services would be limited because of Chad's inability to pay the lawyer's regular fee. His first in-person meeting with Chad was during the custody hearing. Jamie's mother testified that Chad was violent (which he wasn't) and shared the fabricated story of when he attacked Jamie and was arrested. The judge found that Jamie—who was still living with her mother—had a more stable home for Whitney, while Chad did not. Due in part to the attorney's lack of preparation, Chad lost custody of Whitney and was ordered to pay child support to Jamie. Defeated and heartbroken, Chad resigned himself to once-a-month visitation until he could find a new attorney to appeal the case. However, Jamie refused to comply with the visitation order most of the time.

Chad tried to learn everything he could about family law. He asked anyone he knew about his rights. Unfortunately, the people he had access to were mostly people in poverty or health and social workers who knew little or nothing about his legal rights. None of them knew how to guide him through the legal system. In addition, most of the resources for people in poverty are set up for women, so Chad was facing additional barriers trying to get his legal needs met.

Around this time, Chad was diagnosed with stage-4 breast cancer. Although he was homeless with Mark and living in his car, he had surgery and began radiation and chemotherapy treatments. While he was hospitalized and undergoing treatments, his sister took care of Mark. At this time, Jamie was refusing to let him see his daughter but would let Whitney talk on the phone. But as Chad grew sicker, he could not even make phone calls.

When Chad was released from the hospital after his surgery, a social worker helped him to find and move into his own apartment using some funds from a cancer charity. He called both of his children every day. When he started to feel better, he begged Jamie to let him visit Whitney. Jamie finally said he could have a two-hour visit with Whitney at her mother's home. When he arrived, the first thing he noticed was bruises on Whitney. He asked Whitney about the bruises and Whitney said that her mom's new boyfriend hit her. When Jamie heard this, she told him the visit was over and shoved a handful of papers at him. That is when Chad learned that, while he was undergoing chemotherapy, Jamie's mother had helped her file for custody of Whitney.

Afraid for his daughter's safety, Chad called child welfare to report what Whitney had told him. They told him they would investigate. At this point, the cancer and treatments were taking a toll on him. Trembling, sick, and near the breaking point, he went back to legal aid to get help, but was again told that there was a wait list. Chad used every ounce of him strength to call private attorneys from the phone book. He showed up at law firms and begged to see an attorney. He was at his wit's end. It showed in his shaking hands, his face gaunt from chemotherapy, and his thin body. He had clothes from a clothing closet that were too big and he had to keep pulling his pants up. He was turned down time and time again.

It took Chad several months to find a private attorney to help him. This attorney asked him to gather all his paperwork and documentation of everything that had happened since his case went to court. Chad was so sick he could barely make it to the bathroom, let alone locate ALL the paperwork. The attorney quit because Chad was not "following through." During this time, Whitney's mother limited his visitations to phone calls when she "felt" like letting Whitney talk. Weeks went by without any connection to his daughter. A couple of months after being dismissed by his last attorney, Chad was finally assigned to your caseload.

Discussion/Reflection Questions

1. Now that you know more of Chad's story, has your opinion of him changed?

2. Now that you have more information, do you have different assumptions about why Chad might miss or be late for his appointments?

3. Now that you know a bit more about the stresses causing Chad to have problems with finding and bringing in his paperwork, how might you assist him with this?

4. Because of your interactions with Chad, has that changed the way you plan to represent him? How?

5. What more would you like to know in order to understand what's going on in his life and to better serve him? What questions might you ask at the next appointment in order to better represent him?

6. What legal expertise might you apply to assist him in gaining visitation rights?

7. What community resources might you help Chad access?

Defining Poverty and Understanding Its Impacts on Justice

MODULE 2

DEFINING POVERTY AND UNDERSTANDING ITS IMPACTS ON JUSTICE: THE EXPERIENCES OF THOSE IN POVERTY IN OUR SOCIETY AND IN OUR LEGAL SYSTEM

Learning Objectives:

- Understand how lack of knowledge about poverty and its impacts on people prevents legal professionals from meeting the legal needs of those who live in the crisis of poverty.

- Name some facts about poverty in America, including the current minimum wage in your state.

- Describe how people living in poverty often experience the justice system, including law enforcement, and how that differs from the middle-class experience.

- Describe the financial reality of living in poverty and its impacts on access to legal services.

- Name why working hard is not enough to achieve economic stability, and the two variables that can change that.

- Describe four life experiences called "poverty" and the different impact of each on access to legal services.

- Understand the intersections of race and poverty and the danger of calling poverty a race issue.

Video Length: 49 Minutes

POVERTY

We cannot truly begin to address poverty barriers to equal justice without having a clear definition of what we are talking about when we say the word "poverty." In this section, we will explore some of the types of poverty that impact access to justice.

OUR DAILY EXPERIENCES SHAPE WHO WE ARE

Do you have a roof over your head or are you worried about the police putting an eviction notice on your door? Do you have nutritious foods, or are you eating the inexpensive foods that stretch the furthest (but also cause heart disease and obesity)? Do you have educated parents and grandparents or are you being raised by parents who dropped out of school to earn money to help their families? Do you have a doctor or a dentist or do you use super glue to deaden the nerves of your hurting teeth? Do you attend a privileged school or a school with most of the children facing poverty? Do you shop at the only convenience store for miles around or do you shop at a luxury market with the freshest of vegetables? Do you have blankets and clean towels? Do you worry about the water and electricity being shut off?

The daily experiences that we have will shape our expectations and how we see the world. People experiencing poverty have a very different reality than do those who have their Maslow Hierarchy needs met.

Poverty Realities

www.combarriers.com

Norms are developed by your daily life experiences. Isolation perpetuates poverty.

Communication
Across Barriers

Communication
Across Barriers

Poverty Realities

www.combarriers.com

Constant crisis: People are sick more, responding to crises, and in survival mode.

Communication
Across Barriers

Communication
Across Barriers

www.combarriers.com

Communication
Across Barriers

Danny Born Healthy!

Thanks to people bringing resources into our lives: Community Action, Head Start, WIC, legal aid, and stable housing.

Work to understand and build in supports for people who live in the war zone of poverty.

Communication
Across Barriers

www.combarriers.com

Communication
Across Barriers

Reasons for Incarceration

- Failure to pay child support
- Digging in dumpsters for cans/bottles
- Breaking into a camping store
- Failure to pay fines for no car insurance
- Outstanding tickets
- Writing a bad check
- Burglary

Communication
Across Barriers

Poverty Realities

Things get taken away.
People get taken away,
but they are all you have.

FAMILY LOYALTY...
- I love my family.
- They love me.

"He's my brother."

LEGAL BEEGLE ACTIVITY

Legal Beegle

What's the Why Behind Behavior...
Interactions with Law Enforcement (#1)

For one minute, reflect on what you would do if approached by a police officer if you had grown up in generational poverty (where family members were often taken away, where eviction notices were often posted on your door, etc.).

LEGAL BEEGLE ACTIVITY

Legal Beegle

What's the Why Behind Behavior...
Interactions with Law Enforcement (#2)

For one minute, reflect on what you would do if approached by a police officer if you had grown up in a middle-class family (where police officers were seen as friends or people who serve and protect you).

Our experiences shape how we respond to others. What can you do to better interact with clients who have negative experiences with legal or law enforcement professionals?

www.combarriers.com

Communication
Across Barriers

Types of Poverty

- Generational Poverty
- Working-Class Poverty
- Immigrant Poverty
- Situational Poverty

Communication
Across Barriers

TYPES OF POVERTY

To begin to understand experiences of people in poverty, we must start with an explanation of what that word means! One of the most common usages of the word "poverty" comes from the federal government's poverty guidelines. These guidelines determine who is eligible for government services such as legal aid and food stamps. Today, the federal poverty guidelines for a family of four are $24,250. Do a quick back-of-the-envelope calculation of rent, utilities, health care, food, clothes, school supplies, and other basics and you will see the difficulty of surviving on that income. The formula used to calculate what a family of four needs in 2015 is based on a 1960s cost of living. It does not include childcare, transportation, or health care as family needs. The Economic Policy Institute added in cost of childcare, transportation, and health care and determined a family of four would need a minimum of $48,000 just to cover basic human needs in today's society.

While we have these guidelines, we do not have a consensus on what "poverty" is, either at a federal policy level or among the general public. For instance, people experiencing generations of homelessness, illiteracy, and hunger can carry the same "poverty" label as someone who grew up with safe housing, a good education, and a stable family who slips into poverty because of a health crisis or divorce. Both situations are called "poverty," but people in situational poverty have some critical assets. They often have a family safety net and are in a much better position to navigate the courts, which are set up for people who can read and write and have a basic understanding of the legal system. People from generational poverty are less likely to trust the system or know how to navigate it.

In addition to the faulty federal poverty guidelines, we get even more confused because there is no single "poverty" experience. Some people you serve may be experiencing generational poverty, while others may be experiencing working-class poverty, immigrant poverty, situational poverty, or mixed-class poverty. Each of these life experiences is different and shapes our expectations, knowledge, confidence, and opportunities. Understanding the different types of poverty can empower you to better understand and meet your clients where they are. This will improve communication and client follow-through. Below are some characteristics of four lived experiences of poverty.

Generational Poverty

- Are typically workers of the land, as opposed to owners of the land
- May never have connected meaningfully with anyone who benefited from education
- Have not known anyone who was promoted or was respected in a job
- Are highly mobile, often without a home and moving frequently looking for ways to make money
- Have high family illiteracy
- Subconsciously have come to believe that something is wrong with them and that is why they are in poverty
- Learn not to trust professionals or people with titles
- Have likely had negative experiences in trying to access the legal system
- Focus on making it through the day

Working-Class Poverty

- Work, but are barely able to pay for basic needs (no money for any extras)
- Are typically renters as opposed to homeowners
- Often live paycheck to paycheck
- Rarely have health care coverage
- Focus on making it two weeks or through the month
- Learn not to trust people who are making it
- View poverty as personal deficiency

Immigrant Poverty

- Have few or no resources
- Face language and culture barriers

- Seem to have a stronger sense of self than those in working-class and generational poverty

- Often do better than those born into poverty in America

- View poverty as a system problem

Situational Poverty

- Grew up in stable environments and had their basic needs met and more

- Attended school regularly; had health care, family vacations, etc.

- Were surrounded by educated people with living-wage jobs

- Do not recognize advantages of growing up middle class

- Have had a crisis (health, divorce, etc.) and had income and savings drop

- Became isolated (or isolated themselves) from middle-class friends during their poverty crisis

- Are embarrassed by their situation

- Have likely had positive experiences with accessing legal services, but once in poverty, face barriers to equal justice

- Have not internalized poverty as personal deficiency

- Are more likely to make it back into the middle class

Again, the key point here is that the word "poverty" is used to describe many lived experiences, not a monolithic one. This knowledge will empower you to listen to your clients better and gain insight to better address individual barriers that might prevent them from receiving equal access to justice.

These four general types of poverty give a context to your clients' worldviews, expectations, motivations, and communication. And to make things a bit more complicated, there are many more poverty contexts than these four. For instance, a client may be from a mixed-class experience, such as growing up with one parent from the lower middle class and the other from a working-class background, or having one parent from immigrant poverty and the other from situational poverty. These mixed-class experiences influence people's lives in ways that are different from having two parents from a middle-class context.

SOCIAL CLASS CONTEXT SHAPES WORLDVIEW

We learn about our world and develop attitudes, beliefs, and values from our daily life experiences. If your family struggles with hunger, your daily life experiences will be shaped by that. If your family owns their home, your daily life experiences will be impacted by that. If you watch people you love do without their basic needs, you will be affected by that. Every adult who comes into the life of a child is handing that child a description of the world. People can only teach and model what they have been exposed to in a relevant and meaningful way.

> **Example:** The ways that you bathe, eat, dress, talk, and laugh are all taught by the people you have meaningful relationships with.

> **Example:** The way that you believe others should behave is based on your expectations from your own learned norms.

> **Example:** The ways that you celebrate holidays, such as Christmas, Thanksgiving, or Halloween, all relate to your experiences in your context. You learned through communication from those around you how to "be" and what to "expect" on those days.

SOCIAL CLASS CONTEXT SHAPES WORLDVIEW

Exercises: The following activities will assist you in better understanding your own social class experience and how it shapes your actions and worldview.

List three behaviors that were considered normal in your socioeconomic experiences. For example, in my context of generational poverty, we learned to get food quickly and take too much. If we did not do these behaviors, the food would be gone and we would go hungry. In a middle-class context, people are taught to wait for others to get their food and take small amounts because you can always go back for more.

Three behaviors that I learned from my socioeconomic experience are:
1.

2.

3.

Describe how these behaviors may or may not make sense in another social class context.

SOCIAL CLASS CONTEXT SHAPES WORLDVIEW (cont.)

Complete the following sentences:
In my social class context growing up, it was "normal" to...

The oddest thing that I have seen someone from another context do is...

One thing that I have seen somebody from another social class context do that I wouldn't mind having as a part of my worldview is...

Write about some ways behavior defined as normal in your social class context may have directed or limited your life.

Reflect for two minutes on how your social class experiences shape your interactions with your clients.

The Impacts of Poverty

www.combarriers.com

Communication
Across Barriers

• Hopelessness

• Purpose of education or job unclear

• Isolation from middle-class norms, vocabulary, and experiences

• Stereotypes, myths, and judgments

• Internalized personal deficiency

• Poverty realities pull and demand attention

• Sees attorneys as "other"

Communication
Across Barriers

THE WORLDVIEW TAUGHT BY POVERTY

People living in poverty internalize the messages sent their way by society. Families living in the crisis of poverty receive societal messages that they do not belong and they are the cause of their own poverty. Many people come to believe that something is wrong with them. Poverty steals their hope and self-confidence.

Here are some of the messages that people experiencing generational, working-class, and immigrant poverty absorb from society:

• Everyone else is smarter than I am.

• People who are not in poverty are better than I am.

• People who are making it do not care about me.

• I/we don't belong anywhere.

• People like us do not get educated.

• We don't have what we need to break out of poverty.

• There is no one to help.

FACTS ABOUT POVERTY

The Numbers: Far too many people, mostly children, suffer from poverty conditions. More than 14 percent of the population—45.3 million Americans—lives in poverty (U.S. Census Bureau, 2014). Research shows that it is very difficult for people born into poverty to achieve an education and earn a living wage.

Housing: One in four working households in America—10.6 million families—spends more than half of its pre-tax income on housing. This is a level that experts say is unhealthy as well as impossible to sustain. In February 2012, the National Low Income Housing Coalition conducted a study that examined the cost of housing across the United States and found that no city had rentals priced low enough where a minimum-wage earner could reasonably afford to pay rent and have enough money to live comfortably. In 86 percent of counties surveyed, even those who earned twice the minimum wage still did not earn enough money to pay rent and provide for their basic needs.

Welfare: Government assistance falls short of covering basic needs. Many people cling to it because they see no options for earning money for survival with their limited skills, education, and literacy levels. Nationally, the average welfare check for one parent and two children is $478 per month. Thirty years ago, it was $408. Nationally, the average amount added for a baby born to a family already on welfare is $60. However, 23 states offer no additional cash supports when a baby is born to a family on welfare. The average disability check is $756. While people often complain about all the money government gives to people in poverty, the reality is that less than 2 percent of the federal budget is allocated for welfare.

Food: The United States hunger rate continues to be extremely high for an industrialized nation. Many people think hunger does not exist because of obesity. The fact is 46 million people suffer food insecurity and one-third of this group experiences chronic hunger. A person on food stamps receives a total of $4.41 per day. Healthy food is expensive!

Working Hard: In spite of our cultural belief that if people work hard they will do well, many people are working hard and still not making it. According to the 2012 report by Bureau of Labor Statistics, 10.6 million individuals were among the "working poor."

This is a photo of a load of cardboard my brother (who has autism) loaded. He was paid $75 for the load, which took him four days' work to get. So many people are doing hard physical labor but cannot afford a place to live.

Education: Youths living in poverty are the least likely to become educated in our nation. Lack of housing stability and lack of connections to people who have educational success both result in low academic achievement. Families living in poverty often experience education as "stress" and see schools as places where they do not belong. A college education can help people break the barriers of poverty and escape its hardships. Yet, today, it is less likely that a person in poverty will attain a college education than it was in the 1940s.

Effects of Poverty: Many people have internalized poverty as a personal deficiency. Because we do not teach about root causes of poverty (such as lack of access to affordable housing; living-wage jobs; mental, physical, and dental care; adequate nutrition; reliable transportation; and legal services), people come to believe there is something wrong with them and they are the "cause" of poverty. Many see no hope for anything but an insufficient welfare or disability check, or underground activities that barely pay enough to keep food on the table and often result in incarceration. Nearly 80 percent of people in prison cannot read at an eighth-grade level. Poverty affects educational success, health, relationships, and equal access to legal services. Most of all, it affects the ability of humans to develop to their full potential and give back to our communities.

Attitudes: If you watched your grandma go without her medicine, might you get an attitude? If you saw your mom go into an agency and ask for help, only to find plastic or glass separating her from the social worker and a sign saying there was a four-hour wait, might you develop a smart mouth? People are responding to the context of poverty. Effective communication and service requires that you understand that there are reasons for the attitude and smart mouth. It is not about you. If you take it personally, you become defensive and communication breaks down. Give people the benefit of the doubt that there is a good reason for their attitudes. Ask people to help you understand what is going on. Your solutions and services will better meet people where they are and people in poverty will have increased access to justice.

POVERTY IMPACTS ON ACCESS TO JUSTICE

The law and judicial system are designed around the needs of those in wealth and the middle class, with often invisible consequences to those in poverty, such as the following:

In many states, people who do not have a home address cannot legally stay overnight in a federal or state park or sleep on the streets. They are arrested and spend the night in jail.

People who are illiterate or disabled often try to supplement their income to survive. But they are often charged with theft when they dig into dumpsters for bottles to return for deposit or newspapers to recycle for money.

People in poverty who get released from prison often find it impossible to obtain housing and employment. Yet, they receive letters saying they must pay for parole supervision or pay to maintain a website listing their crime and their personal information.

People who cannot pay rent are evicted and forced to attend "ready to rent" courses.

People on welfare who sign up for higher education or training are sanctioned in all but five states. They are told they cannot go to school or get training because they must be available to accept any minimum-wage job that might be offered, and, if they are in classes, they are not able to accept the jobs offered. However, research shows a person with a high school diploma or less has a limited chance of earning a living wage or of moving up in the American labor market.

People who live on a limited income, one that does not even cover rent and utilities, often get their driver's licenses suspended for not making payments on fines for driving uninsured.

Most places in America do not have transportation systems to get people where they need to be. Those in poverty have to be more places, as they are complying with agencies and trying to get their basic needs met.

Children in families facing homelessness and hunger are taken away from parents for poverty, not neglect.

People in poverty are told to "go get paperwork, go to drug treatment, show up" when they have no resources or capacity to follow through.

SOME FACTS ON THE HISTORY OF POVERTY

Most people do not know that it was a crime in England to be poor. People were sentenced to indentured servitude in America. Many emerged from indentured servitude without literacy or skills to earn a living wage. They worked the land but did not earn enough to be landowners.

In Pennsylvania in the 1700s, there was a law that said, "If you are poor and cannot take care of your family, you must wear a P on your sleeve when you leave your home. It must be four inches in height and be red or blue." In the notes regarding this law, people wrote, "If we can humiliate people enough, they will quit acting poor." Much of our response to people in poverty today is founded on this historical belief. Can you think of a policy that is founded on this historical belief: If we can make it hard enough on them, if we can be tough enough, they will stop acting poor?

The way we label people shapes how we treat people. Some of the most common labels we have used historically to describe people living in the deepest poverty in America include "the dangerous class," "the underclass," "the hard to serve," "riff raff" and "trash."

POVERTY CROSSES RACE

Poverty is often perceived as a race or ethnic issue. It is commonly described as a problem that is associated with racism. Actually, some minorities are indeed overrepresented among those in poverty, but not all. Compared with an overall poverty rate of 15.1 percent, for example, 27.4 percent of Blacks were categorized as "poor" in 2010, and 26.6 percent in that same category were Hispanic. For Asians, however, the figure was 12.1 percent. This compares with a poverty rate of 9.9 percent for Whites (National Poverty Center, 2010). In total numbers, though, it is important to note that the majority (close to 41 percent) of people in poverty in the United States are White, with a total number of over 26 million in 2012 (Kaiser Family Foundation, 2012).

Research studies on poverty often ignore the White people in poverty. Educational and public service professionals and organizations frame their services in a manner that does not account for the unique needs and situations of White people in poverty. Poverty needs to be acknowledged as a large-scale societal problem that cuts across racial/ethnic lines, and special attention should be paid to the voices and needs of those in poverty who have often been marginalized, ignored, and treated as invisible.

Number in Poverty and Poverty Rates by Race/Ethnicity, 2012		
Race/Ethnicity	Number	Poverty Rate
All races	62,498,000	19.8%
White	26,223,200	13%
Black	13,027,600	35%
Hispanic (of any race)	17,717,000	33%
Source: Kaiser Family Foundation, 2012		

Link to the Eyes on the Prize Video Series:
(www.pbs.org/wgbh/amex/eyesontheprize/)

CASE STUDY!

UNDERSTANDING THE IMPACT OF POVERTY ON CHAD'S LIFE

At your next meeting, you ask Chad to tell you a bit more about himself. From what he tells you, you learn quite a bit more about his story.

Chad was raised in extreme poverty. His mother could not read or write, and his father was barely literate. Chad lived out of a car most of his life. Because of Chad's family's mobile lifestyle, Chad barely attended school during his elementary years and dropped out partway through middle school. Because of this, he could read a few words, but could not read a newspaper. His writing ability was limited.

Chad met Shannon—a girl from his neighborhood who was also raised in chronic poverty—when they were both in middle school. They began their relationship and Chad soon fell in love! Shannon's home life was very stressful. Her mom had a string of abusive boyfriends that would take out their anger and their desires on both Shannon and her mom. Shannon used alcohol and drugs to hide from the pain that these men caused in her life. Before they were even 15 years old, Chad and Shannon had moved out of their families' homes and tried to find a place to live together. Because they both were middle-school dropouts, it was hard for them to find jobs that would provide them enough money to survive. They were often homeless, sleeping in their car or moving between friends' homes. Even though Shannon wanted to escape her past and leave the drugs and alcohol behind, the stresses of poverty and the lack of resources to help her with her addictions kept her trapped.

Because of Shannon's addiction to drugs, she and Chad had a long, on-again/off-again relationship. He loved her dearly and wanted to protect and provide for her. But the drugs were too powerful for Shannon to overcome. Even after the birth of their son, Mark, Shannon still struggled with drugs. She loved Chad and Mark so much, but the drugs kept pulling her back into a life she did not want. She finally decided that Mark was better off without her—so she left Mark with Chad when Mark was about three years old.

After Shannon left, Chad and Mark moved into a car that Chad had bought at an auction for $50. Chad spent a few dollars to get it running, but that would not last long. Something else would eventually go wrong with the car and they would be stranded somewhere. At one point, the car was towed for lack of insurance and he had no money to retrieve it. Thus, he was forced to drop out of a job training program that he had just gotten into because he had no transportation to get there.

Chad eventually found a minimum-wage job. That is where he met Jamie. The three of them soon moved in together and Chad and Jamie eventually married. Even through both were employed, they found it hard to make enough money to cover the household bills and even more difficult to afford any extras. When Jamie ran out of birth control pills, they had no way to get to a clinic and no money to pay for the prescription. Jamie got pregnant and they soon had a beautiful baby girl they named Whitney. At first, they were so happy that Whitney had joined their small family. But not too long after they moved to Phoenix with Jamie's mom, things got bad. After a four-year relationship, Chad was thrown out and Jamie and her mother took Whitney.

It was about this time that Chad got hurt on the job. Because he was "working under the table," there was no worker's compensation to cover the doctor visit. But the pain was radiating around his chest, so he figured he should go visit the only doctor he had ever known: "the emergency room." After what seemed like an extremely invasive examination, the ER doctor told Chat that he probably just had a pulled muscle and a few internal bruises. But he advised Chad to go see his regular physician because there was an unusual mass near his breast that should be double checked. Chad left with a couple pain pills and a prescription for more, which he of course could not afford to fill. Chad went home and rested for a couple of days. That was the easy part, because they "let him go" due to his on-the-job injury. He never gave the "unusual mass" a second thought.

Chad continued to find minimum-wage work but never earned enough to afford the stability of a home. He and Mark survived day by day. Even though he hoped for a better life for Mark, he was teaching Mark the same things that his father had taught him. Mark rarely went to school and was eager to drop out and find a job of his own.

During a couple more visits to the emergency room, Chad was again advised to see his personal physician because of the unusual mass near his breast. But Chad had never had a personal physician, did not have health insurance, and shrugged off any thoughts about the mass in his breast. Occasionally, when showering or stretching, Chad would feel the lump. He often wondered why it was still there and why it felt like it was growing, but did not worry about it. Occasionally, he would curse himself for being so clumsy and letting that piece of pipe hit him on the chest like that.

A couple of years later, when the lump was visible in the bathroom mirror, Chad decided he needed to return to the emergency room and have them check it out again. He was stunned – and humiliated – when he was diagnosed with stage-4 breast cancer. He was only 38 years old— "and a man, seriously?"

Discussion/Reflection Questions

1. What do you see as the "causes" of poverty in Chad's story?

2. What type of poverty did Chad grow up in?

3. How do you think Chad's past has contributed to his world-view of legal professionals (and other helping professionals)—and has contributed to his frustration and stress?

4. Chad received some government/legal assistance during his story. Reflect on how the assistance helped or did not help.

5. At what points in Chad's experience could he have benefited from legal advice?

6. If you were Chad's attorney sooner in his story, what steps could you have taken to improve his legal outcomes?

7. Could earlier legal interventions have made a difference for Chad's medical situation? For Shannon's drug issues and her relationship with Mark?

8. How might Chad's outcomes been different had he been female?

www.combarriers.com

Examining Assumptions About Poverty

Communication
Across Barriers

What do you believe about poverty and those who live in it?

Communication
Across Barriers

MODULE 3

EXAMINING ASSUMPTIONS ABOUT POVERTY: HOW UNIVERSAL ACCESS TO JUSTICE DEPENDS ON LEGAL PROFESSIONALS BEING ABLE TO SEE AND SUSPEND JUDGMENTS OF "OTHERS"

Learning Objectives:

- Understand how stereotypes and myths reduce our ability to provide equal justice.

- Learn why it's common to impose blame and judgment when we see the choices of people in poverty.

- Describe specific ways that judging clients in poverty can cripple effective communication.

- Develop awareness of unconscious bias and how bias can lead to decisions about whom we will assist and whom we will not help.

- Gain "active listening" skills including the ability to suspend thoughts or judgments that prevent understanding the perspectives and strengths of your clients.

- Learn why communicating with someone from a different background can cause misunderstandings and leave clients not knowing what to do next.

- Describe root causes of poverty.

- Understand how the need to "belong" drives motivation and choices that are often judged by those not in poverty.

Video Length: 14 Minutes

WHAT MOST OF AMERICA IS TAUGHT ABOUT POVERTY

Think about where you get your information on poverty. If you are like others, it is from television and newspapers. The number-one teacher of poverty in America is the media! However, the media tends to dramatize, sensationalize, and present extreme cases, resulting in deeply embedded stereotypes of poverty in our society. Facts about the real causes of and solutions to poverty are rarely presented, and therefore most people remain unaware of the realities of poverty, even in their own communities.

We do an inadequate job in this country teaching people about poverty. Universities graduate future teachers, counselors, lawyers, judges, researchers, politicians, and other professionals without them ever learning about poverty. Few Americans have had the course "The History of Poverty in the United States." We do not know our history. We do not know models used to address poverty or how we have come to our current understanding of poverty. The implications of this lack of poverty education are devastating. It fosters stereotypes with the general public and creates leaders and decision makers who have little or no real understanding of poverty or its impacts on people. It results in programs, policies, and procedures that do not work to move people out of poverty but rather punish them and exacerbate poverty.

Before we can work more effectively with people living in poverty, we must make a collective effort to examine personal beliefs and open our minds to new interpretations of the behavior of those struggling without basic needs. Attitudes and beliefs shape tone of voice, body posture, facial expressions, and actions toward others which, in turn, determines the communication and behavioral strategies of those we interact with. Our judgments impede connection and understanding. Therefore, we need to reflect on our beliefs.

Questions to reflect on:

- What images come to your mind when you hear the word "poverty"?

- What do you believe causes poverty?

- Where do your beliefs come from (e.g., your parents, environment, community, media, personal experience, etc.)?

- Were your experiences and opportunities different from those of the people struggling in poverty whom you serve?

- Do you know the facts about poverty in your community?

- Are you able to suspend judgment and believe that people are making the best decisions possible from their perspective?

- Are you willing to provide legal assistance to people who may believe and respond differently than you?

LEGAL BEEGLE ACTIVITY

Legal Beegle

Assumptions

Take a few seconds to reflect on the first things you think about when you see someone with rotten teeth or no teeth. Where did the ideas you reflected on come from?

LEGAL BEEGLE ACTIVITY

Legal Beegle

The Impact of Assumptions

We make assumptions based on our individual lived experiences combined with social programming from the country we grow up in, the geographic region we live in, the social institutions that we intersect with, and our families of origin. For the next few minutes, reflect on the following questions:

1. What do you believe about poverty and the people who live in it?

2. Where did you get your information?

3. How does it impact whom you go out of your way for, whom you believe in, whom you are willing to hear?

LEGAL BEEGLE ACTIVITY

Legal Beegle

Interpretation and Active Listening

Read the story below about the wealthy Native American woman and follow the directions on the next page to answer the questions. This is a timed activity. You have two minutes to complete your task.

After two minutes, debrief with another (if possible) and reach a consensus on the correct answers. Then, review the answer sheet and reflect on why you believe you chose the answers you chose.

A Wealthy Native American Woman

A wealthy Native American woman had just opened the door to her car when a middle-class African American man appeared and demanded money. The passenger opened the purse. The contents fell to the ground. The man took the money and left. The wealthy Native American woman called the poor White parking garage attendant.

Legal Beegle

From your recollection,
mark true, false, or unknown next to each statement in regard to the story you just read/heard.

	True	False	Unknown
1. The wealthy Native American woman opened her purse.	☐	☐	☐
2. The purse contained money.	☐	☐	☐
3. The wealthy Native American woman had opened the door to her car.	☐	☐	☐
4. The middle-class African American man was a thief.	☐	☐	☐
5. The poor White parking garage attendant was the man at the car door.	☐	☐	☐
6. The middle-class African American man took the contents of the purse.	☐	☐	☐
7. There was a man inside the car.	☐	☐	☐
8. The middle-class African American man took the money.	☐	☐	☐
9. The wealthy Native American woman owned the car.	☐	☐	☐
10. The middle-class African American man was a passenger.	☐	☐	☐

Answers found in Appendix A, page 127.

ACTIVE LISTENING

Hearing is done with the ear.
Listening is done with the mind.

How would you rate yourself as a listener?
        Superior   Good   Poor

How do you think your clients would rate you as a listener?
        Superior   Good   Poor

When are you hearing, but not listening?

1. Pseudo-listening: Your mind is on other things.

2. Stage hogging: You are only interested in sharing your ideas.

3. Selective listening: You respond only to parts of the conversation that are of interest to you.

SEVEN STRATEGIES TO IMPROVE ACTIVE LISTENING WITH YOUR CLIENTS

1. Keep your mind open: Suspend judgment and give people the benefit of the doubt that whatever they are doing or saying makes sense from their perspective.

2. Listen for ideas you can build on.

3. Resist distractions.

4. Be curious.

5. Words are symbols. Meanings are in people. Ask clarifying questions to ensure shared meaning.

6. Mentally summarize what your client says.

7. Verbally state key points of what you hear and ask your client if that is what she or he meant.

CASE STUDY!

MOVING BEYOND ASSUMPTIONS ABOUT CHAD

After more conversations with Chad, you learn more of his story and discover some of his strengths.

Chad was a hard worker. He would work long hours at physically demanding jobs to provide for his family. He would accept jobs for meager pay, just to say he was employed. He would work under the table and without benefits, just to be able to bring home some money.

Even when Chad was unemployed or not involved in a training program, he was always trying to do things to help his family survive. He was mechanically inclined which came in handy for fixing any broken-down car. He was able to get most folks' cars running—without a lot of money for parts. He was so creative and resourceful. He knew how to improvise and make do with whatever he had to fix a car. Sometimes he would make a couple of bucks from helping a friend out; sometimes he would just help a friend out!

Chad has many skills and talents. He was great at repairing electronic equipment and appliances. If something broke, he was the one people went to. He often would find a television or stereo that someone had thrown away and make it work. Sometimes he could sell these things for a profit; sometimes he would give them to someone to make their life a bit better.

Chad was also an exceptional father and caregiver. He cared so much for Mark and wanted to provide a great home for him. It was awesome to see him playing with Mark while Mark was just a toddler. He taught him how to play with a ball. He would often spend hours with him at a park and help him go down the slide and push him on the swing. You could hear their laughter ring out throughout the playground. The same could be said about his feelings for Whitney. When they were together, he was a loving and caring father. She knew that her daddy loved and adored her. Even when Jamie was withholding visitation—and when

Chad had the extra resources—he would support Whitney in whatever way he could: buying diapers, occasionally picking up a new toy or outfit for her, and dropping food off at Jamie's mother's house.

Chad was also the entertainer in his family. He could pick a 12-string guitar like no one else. He taught his brothers and Mark to play the guitar. He also loved to sing. Because of him, there was always music in his house. When poverty experiences hit the family really hard, he would sing! Chad could also tell some of the funniest jokes and made everyone laugh—even when it seemed like there was nothing to laugh about. He kept the family together through homelessness, hunger, and other hardships presented by a life time of poverty.

Discussion/Reflection Questions

1. Now that you have had a few "meetings" with Chad and know a bit more about him, how have your assumptions changed?

2. What do you see as Chad's strengths?

3. What have you learned by getting to know Chad that can help you gct to know your future clients better?

4. In what ways can you improve your listening skills to be better able to get to know your clients?

Improving Communication Across Poverty Barriers

MODULE 4

IMPROVING COMMUNICATION ACROSS POVERTY BARRIERS: OVERCOMING OTHER BARRIERS TO EQUAL JUSTICE WHEN SERVING PEOPLE FROM POVERTY

Learning Objectives:

- Name five common reasons why communication between a legal professional and a client in poverty might break down.

- Share three levels of self-disclosure in communication and which level builds trust between legal professionals and clients.

- Describe how to create common ground and build identification to improve communication across poverty barriers.

- Explain how word of mouth (oral culture) styles of communicating and relating differ from literate (print culture) styles of communicating and how the differences can cause misunderstandings.

- Describe the importance of sharing the "why" behind your actions.

- List some specific communication strategies legal professionals can use to communicate more effectively with clients who are more oral culture communicators.

Video Length: 28 Minutes

IMPROVING COMMUNICATION ACROSS BARRIERS

Communication is complex even when we are interacting with people with similar backgrounds and life experiences, and the complexities grow when we interact with those from different backgrounds and experiences. This session will provide tools to support mutual understanding when communicating with clients living in poverty and supply strategies for establishing trusting and productive relationships.

IDENTIFICATION—A KEY INGREDIENT TO COMMUNICATION

Identification: When people see how they are "like" each other, it builds common ground and improves communication. One very important basis of identification is values. We are attracted to people who have similar values and who see the world the way that we do. We might consider people weird if they have values that are different than our own.

Building identification requires self-disclosure. There are three common levels of self-disclosure: 1) Sharing information (most attorneys communicate with clients at this level); 2) Sharing information and something that builds common ground; and 3) Telling clients all of your problems so that the conversation becomes about you.

You do not have to self-disclose at level three to build identification, but you do have to go to level two of self-disclosure to build relationships and improve communication. Share things about yourself that assist clients in seeing you are just a person, not so different than they are. This type of sharing can build trust and improve follow-through.

It is easy to build common ground with our fellow human beings. We are more alike than we are different. All humans have the same feelings. If you share you are feeling overwhelmed or happy, your client can relate. You can build common ground based on the number and/or type of siblings you have or the type of ice cream you like. Identification is when your client sees how she or he is like you and you see how you are like your client.

Example: When we are talking to somebody new, we may ask her if she likes a new movie or play that we have recently seen. If she says "yes" and we liked it too, we have a sense of identification with her.

Example: Rich and privileged politicians often stress their real or non-real likeness to common people, building identification. One example would be a very wealthy president who stressed his enjoyment of country music.

LEGAL BEEGLE ACTIVITY

Legal Beegle

Identification Activity

Make a list of people you identify with.

1.
2.
3.
4.
5.

Now, think of why you identify with them.

Write about what kinds of situations could arise that could cause you to think of them as different and not identify with them. Remember that any two people are both alike and different. How they get along will depend on whether they find the ways in which they are alike and are able to identify with each other.

Think about your clients. What might you share with them to help them identify with you? What can you tune into to see common ground with your clients?

**Five Main Causes of
Communication Breakdown**

- Subconscious bias

- Distrust of outsiders/fear of professionals

- Differences in priorities/worldviews

- Differences in basic communication styles

- Differences in vocabulary and examples

Communication
Across Barriers

THE FIVE MAIN CAUSES OF COMMUNICATION BREAKDOWN

The five main causes of communication breakdown are: 1) Subconscious bias; 2) Distrust of outsiders/ fear of professionals; 3) Differences in priorities/worldviews; 4) Differences in basic communication styles (print- versus oral-culture styles); and 5) Differences in vocabulary and examples. These areas are explored more below. Suggestions for addressing them are provided below in "10 Strategies to Jump-Start Improved Communication."

1) SUBCONSCIOUS BIAS.

Professionals and those from the upper and middle classes have often formed subconscious biases about people in poverty that are often difficult to recognize and overcome. People in poverty also hold biases about people who are not in poverty. These subconscious biases can keep us from understanding each other and hamper efforts to provide legal services. The three main sources of bias about people in poverty come from:

A. Segregation and isolation. Most middle-class people spend time with other people who are middle class. People in poverty tend to be surrounded by others who are in similar situations. This segregation by social class only exposes us to one way of life and does not allow us to understand the circumstances in which other people live.

B. The media. The number-one teacher of poverty in America is the media—which often dramatizes, sensationalizes, and provides extremes that perpetuate stereotypes and myths.

C. The myth of the land of opportunity. The United States has been called "the land of opportunity." People are taught that everyone starts out the same and has the same chances—that every U.S. citizen can achieve success through ability and hard work. Conversely, we are taught that if someone does not succeed, it's her or his fault. We learn that only people who lack ambition, are lazy, or have personal flaws experience poverty in our wealthy country.

2) DISTRUST OF OUTSIDERS/FEAR OF PROFESSIONALS.

People in poverty may have limited exposure to people they can trust from other socio-economic classes and helping professions (including those within the legal system). Their experiences may include overworked and burned-out service providers or government employees who are unable to provide them what they need and who often do not have the communication skills for relating effectively with their clients. Prior experiences in the legal system may have left them feeling afraid, ashamed, judged, and inadequate. If communication with a previous attorney broke down, they may have been punished or judged for not following instructions that they did not understand or did not know how to follow. If they themselves have not had a bad experience, they likely have known someone who has and may feel uneasy and struggle to trust their attorney.

3) DIFFERENCES IN PRIORITIES/WORLDVIEWS.

We all have driving forces behind the decisions we make. The daily life experiences of people living in the crisis of poverty are different from those living in more affluent classes. In poverty, decisions are often made based on survival, relationships, and getting temporary relief from the war zone of poverty. In the upper and middle classes, decisions are often based on family, career success, and material security. What seems possible in the middle-class context may seem impossible in the context of poverty. Understanding that your worldview/priorities may not match those of the people you are serving is a first step to improving communication.

4) DIFFERENCES IN BASIC COMMUNICATION STYLES.

One of the best ways to overcome breakdowns in communication is by understanding the differences in two basic styles of communication: print- and oral-culture communication styles. Walter Ong, the first to identify the impact of poverty and privilege on communication styles, observed that all people are born into oral culture. Over time, they learn to be print culture if they grow up around adults who rely on reading more than talking for gathering and sharing information.

Oral culture does not mean that people cannot read; it means that they prefer to seek information for living their lives from others (through verbal means, not print). One communication style is not inherently better than the other. But, in America, most of our systems, including the legal system, are set up to serve and value those who communicate and relate in a more print-culture style.

Understanding the preferred communication and learning styles of our clients increases our chances to succeed in reaching out to them, establishing relationships, and learning about their strengths, assets, and resiliency characteristics. When legal professionals apply the skills and knowledge of oral and print communication traits in their work, they more effectively serve people in poverty and can empower them to navigate and succeed in middle-class systems. (Traits of oral and print cultures are listed on your copy of the PowerPoint).

5) DIFFERENCES IN VOCABULARY/EXAMPLES.

Legal professionals can often derail communication by speaking in legalese or providing examples from middle-class lifestyles that clients from poverty can't relate to. Without common vocabulary and examples, the information does not make sense, which often leaves the client with little understanding of what she or he is supposed to do next and often no capacity to follow through with attorney instructions.

www.combarriers.com

Improving Communication Across Poverty Barriers

Communication
Across Barriers

Every human being is born oral culture. Oral culture teaches a focus on senses (touch, smell, sight, sound, and taste).

Oral culture is linked to poverty and emphasizes our need for trusting relationships.

Print culture is linked to literacy and is generally used by helping professionals.

Communication
Across Barriers

ORALITY AND LITERACY

Walter Ong (1982) first reported a difference in communication styles (how people received and shared information) based on socioeconomic status in his book *Orality and Literacy*. Ong's worldwide research showed that people living in the crisis of poverty tended to communicate in a more oral, "word-of-mouth" style of communication, while people in a middle-class context tended to communicate in a more literate, print style of communication. These two distinct styles of communicating and relating are based on how individuals receive information. Each style brings rich opportunities for human growth and connections.

All human beings are born oral-culture communicators. It is our natural way to send and receive messages. We learn the middle-class print-culture style of communicating if we are surrounded by people who get their primary information from reading. The ways in which humans send and receive information shape their communication styles.

Oral Culture

- You seek information through relationships.
- You are spontaneous and skilled at having multiple conversations at once.
- Interrupting is okay.
- Repetition and telling the same stories over and over helps in your understanding.
- Sharing personal experiences and stories is your way of connecting with others.
- It is normal to show emotions/feelings.
- You are very physical and expect physical responses.

Communication
Across Barriers

Communication
Across Barriers

Orality is a natural state in which we are highly attuned to our senses (touch, smell, sight, sound, and taste) and devote a great deal of attention to sensory information. Orality emphasizes our interconnection with the environment and the people in it. Some characteristics of orality are spontaneity, connectedness, present orientation, comfort with emotions, ability to see "the big picture," and holistic point of view.

In oral culture (orality), individuals seek information for living their lives by asking others they know and trust. They trust people—not paper—for gaining information. They highly value people with whom they personally identify. There is an unspoken loyalty, and relationships are placed above tasks or objects.

Example: Imagine that you are having a conversation with some- one about planning your future. A beautiful bird lands just a short distance from you. You see the bird and start discussing the color of its feathers, the way it cocks its beak, etc. You have forgotten all about the conversation that was going on. That is orality. That is being present oriented. That is being in the "here and now." If your conversation happens to be with a person who is also from oral culture, that person will understand your changing the sub- ject. If your conversation is with a middle- or upper-class person who is more conditioned by print, she or he may get upset or be uncomfortable with your changing the subject. Oral-culture peo- ple are into what is happening at the time. They are highly sensitive to what is going on around them at all times. They are elemental, hypersensitive, and hyperaware of their environment. They must be to survive.

Example: Our natural style of communicating is orality. As babies and small children, we do not hesitate to cry if we are hurt, or to want what we want when we want it. Children have short atten- tion spans. They do one thing for a short period of time, see something else that they are interested in, and are off to do some- thing else. Children see the world through relationships. Everything is connected. Orality is our natural state. It is respond- ing to the world without thinking through how our responses will be received. Our human nature is to see connections and respond spontaneously to our environments.

Example: An oral culture is one in which the vast majority of the important information forming an individual's worldview comes from speech (storytelling, conversations, etc.). People tend to learn by doing or experiencing through someone else's experi- ences. People who grow up in this environment are natural. You can remain in touch with your natural orality by listening to and trusting your feelings. In order to fully understand oral culture, you have to consider it in comparison with print culture.

Ong found that women of all social classes tended to display more oral-culture communication and learning characteristics. He attributed this to the fact that women had limited access to an education and therefore relied more heavily on word-of-mouth communication. This reliance on verbal communication resulted in people displaying more of the characteristics of oral culture.

Ong also found that people from minority populations tended to exhibit the dominant style of oral culture communication because they, too, relied more on gaining information from people, not paper.

Ong's research showed that people living in poverty, regardless of race or sex, overwhelmingly displayed oral-culture characteristics. Ong discovered that the conditions of poverty created a need for people to communicate using oral skills. For example, in poverty one might acquire material items, but those items are often lost, stolen, repossessed, or taken away. Poverty teaches that people are all you have, which elevates the importance of relationships. Poverty is also unpredictable and chaotic, and people in poverty are constantly addressing one crisis after another. This poverty experience programs people to be flexible and to go with the flow. The spontaneity of oral culture is compatible with the crisis nature of poverty.

www.combarriers.com

Print Culture

Communication
Across Barriers

Literacy is a learned way of relating to the world, where people learn to process and analyze (breaking things down according to parts) information collected through sight, sound, hearing, touch, and smell according to categories, classifications, and styles of reasoning developed by reading.

Communication
Across Barriers

Print Culture

www.combarriers.com

Communication
Across Barriers

- You are a linear thinker and you like things in order...first this, then this, etc.

- You are most comfortable focusing on one idea at a time.

- You believe a plan is essential and your goal is to stay on task.

- It is important to think abstractly about situations and analyze them carefully.

- You approach tasks by breaking them into parts.

Communication
Across Barriers

Print Culture

www.combarriers.com

Communication
Across Barriers

- You sort and categorize information.

- Time is crucial and you are rigid about it.

- You do not show emotions or physical affection unless you know someone really well, and you do not share personal stories.

- When you need information, you look for a book or article on the subject.

Communication
Across Barriers

A print-culture style of communicating and learning comes from reading. If children are surrounded by adults who read for their primary information, they will likely gain the skills of print culture. Print culture is a learned communication style gained through reading as a primary source of information.

Print culture (literacy) is a learned way of relating to the world where people learn to process and analyze (breaking things down according to parts) information collected through sight, sound, hearing, touch, and smell according to categories, classifications, and styles of reasoning developed by reading. Some characteristics of print culture are: self-discipline (ability to not pay attention to everything that is going on around you, but rather to focus on a single idea), separation and disconnection, ability to develop technology, ability to break things down into parts, and ability to organize efforts according to predetermined goals.

> **Example**: Imagine again that you are having a conversation with someone about a legal issue. A beautiful bird lands just a short distance from the window in your office. You see the bird and notice that it is very interesting. But, it is not the subject at hand. So you don't think about the bird anymore. Instead, you continue to focus on the legal issue. This is self-discipline. If your conversation is with a person who is from oral culture, that person may feel hurt and/or rejection that you are so focused on the task and not into relating with them, sharing, and hearing about the bird. If you are talking with someone who is also print-culture oriented, that person will appreciate your ability to stay on task.

> **Example**: When literacy (print) came to the nations of Europe, they developed technology, strategy, and military discipline, which enabled them to take over most of the world, because the oral cultures (such as Indians of the Americas) did not have the combination (developed by print) of intellectual skills that develop technology, strategy, and military organization. The oral cultures fought their battles more spontaneously without thinking through strategies that could have helped them with their struggles.

Example: When you learn to read, you must shut out sense data. You cannot pay attention to other sights, sounds, smells, etc., or you will not understand what you are reading. Reading teaches you to not pay attention to what is going on around you. When you read, you must be focused on what you are reading or you will not understand it. Because letters have no meanings in themselves, the meaning of what we read comes from the ways in which many interchangeable parts (letters) are organized. Therefore, people who are more literate (print oriented) are better at thinking about things according to the parts that make up the whole and at organizing parts into new combinations. You can gain the skills of print culture through reading, making lists, and outlining what you have read.

A BALANCED ORIENTATION

Exercise: There are times when we need to have print-culture orientation. Think of three situations or examples of times when it would be important to have characteristics of print culture such as self-discipline (ability to not pay attention to everything that is going on around you, but rather to focus on a single idea), separation and disconnection, ability to delay gratification, ability to strategize and plan ahead, ability to set goals, ability to develop technology, ability to break things down into parts, or ability to organize efforts according to predetermined goals.

A BALANCED ORIENTATION
(cont.)

Exercise: List five events in your life that you've reacted to without thinking through what you were going to do or say. These are times when you just followed your instincts. Was your response a negative or positive outcome? Are there events where you wish you had thought through your actions and planned ahead? Are there times when it was good that you reacted spontaneously?

LEGAL BEEGLE ACTIVITY

Legal Beegle

What Is Your Dominant Communication Style?

The tool on the next two pages can assist you in exploring your dominant style of communication. It can also provide you with insights for developing strategies to better connect with and serve those you work with.

Instructions: Read each statement on the chart and write your score in the box to the right of the statement. Rate each statement on a scale of 1-5 depending on how much the statement describes your behavior.

1. No. This statement does not describe my style.

2. Mostly Not. This statement is mostly not true for me.

3. Sometimes. Half the time, this statement is true for me.

4. Mostly Yes. This statement captures my style most of the time.

5. Yes. This statement describes my style.

Add the scores in each column on the next two pages.

If the two totals are close to the same number, congratulations! Walter Ong would say you are a balanced communicator. If you have a more than 20 percent higher score in either oral or print communication, examine how you can gain and implement the skills to achieve balance for communicating and relating more effectively.

If you scored higher on oral and lower on print, read the print strategies and begin incorporating them into your communication.

If you scored higher on print and lower on oral, read the oral strategies and begin incorporating them into your communication.

What Is Your Dominant Communication Style?

Legal Beegle

Creating a welcoming environment is a priority. I set the tone by noticing people, and learning their names and interests.	
Relationships are more important than rules or procedures. I put people first.	
I like to have multiple conversations at once.	
I learn best from telling or listening to stories.	
I like to work in groups and socialize and learn from each other; even though it may be noisy from conversations.	
I prefer conversations about people.	
I like frequent reminders.	
In conversations, I pay attention to facial expressions, body posture, and tone of voice more than the content of what is being said.	
I like to touch, try, and experiment when I am learning.	
I have a schedule, but change it according to the situation.	
When I need information for living my life, I'll ask someone I trust who is like me.	
I am physical and expect physical responses.	
I tell everyone just about everything! That's the only way they will really know me.	
Total	

What Is Your Dominant Communication Style?

Legal Beegle

I like to focus on one idea at a time.	
I prefer rules to ambiguity.	
I do not interrupt.	
I want just facts, not story.	
I prefer to work quietly alone.	
I prefer conversations about ideas.	
I approach work by breaking tasks into clear steps.	
I only show emotions and share feelings with people I know really well.	
I believe a plan is essential and my goal is to stay on task.	
In conversations, I focus on the content of what's being said more than the nonverbals and the environment in which it is being said.	
When I need information for living my life, I'll research it and read the information.	
Time is crucial and I am rigid about it.	
I do not share personal stories.	
Total	

What Is Your Dominant Communication Style? (cont)

Legal Beegle

Our communication style shapes how we relate and how we learn. One style is not better than another. In America, we tend to place value on print-culture communication, relating, and learning characteristics. In poverty and in most countries, there is more value placed on the oral-culture style of communicating, relating, and learning. The ideal is to understand the different styles and communicate in a more balanced way.

If you are dominant print culture, you can get back in touch with your natural style of communicating (oral culture) by paying attention to your feelings and following your intuition. If you are more oral culture, you can gain the skills of print culture through reading information that is useful for living your life. A balanced communicator will skillfully use characteristics of each style as appropriate for communicating effectively.

BALANCE

Walter Ong first linked oral-culture communication style with poverty and print-culture communication style with the middle class. These two distinct styles of communication are often at the core of misunderstandings and relationship breakdown. Communication is most effective when we use a balance between the two styles. If you are too dominant in print-culture communication style (one idea at a time, linear, etc.), you may focus so much on the task that you neglect building and maintaining relationships with those you serve. You may also be losing people who are used to multiple ideas and multi-sensory inputs. On the other hand, if you are too dominant with oral-culture communication style, you probably have great rapport with those you work with, but they may not be gaining the print-culture skills they need to succeed in the legal system and the work world.

Balance is the ability to maintain both the characteristics of oral culture (which keep you connected and spontaneous) and the skills of print culture (which allow you to set goals, plan ahead, analyze, and stay focused). Oral culture is our natural way to relate and communicate. Print culture is a learned style of connecting with and relating to others. Ong taught that to fully connect and develop our potential, we need our natural style of oral culture as we master the skills of print culture.

Most legal systems are set up to serve print-culture-dominant communicators. Communication misunderstandings can occur when we are not aware of the two distinct styles of communicating and relating.

> **Example**: If we lose our sense of orality, we lose touch with the people around us and with nature. If we do not have the skills of literacy (print culture), we cannot plan ahead, set goals, and improve our society. We must have a balance between the ability to be analytical and organized on the one hand, and the ability to understand that everything is connected and to be spontaneous on the other hand.

> **Example**: Increasing access to justice across poverty barriers requires valuing the skills of both orality and literacy. You must have strategy and organization, and you also need the ability to respond spontaneously to realities your client is facing in the war zone of poverty. A balanced approach is a better methodology.

> **Example**: Jazz, blues, rock, and folk music come from oral cultures. The musicians provide spontaneous creativity, and their music reflects interaction with the other musicians and with listeners or dancers. Classical and traditional popular music involve less creativity by the players, who try to make the music sound as much as possible like the composer intended. These are musical styles of print culture. Often in the case of great music, there is a balance between the creativity of the composer and arranger and the creativity of the musician and singer.

A BALANCED LEGAL APPROACH

A balanced approach would be when you would use a balance of both the characteristics of orality (spontaneity, comfort with emotion, ability to see our connections to each other and to nature, etc.) and the skills of print culture (organization, analysis, planning ahead, focus, etc.).

An example situation would be working with a client in a civil case. Oral characteristics would promote your ability to relate to and understand the needs of the person you are serving, to keep in mind whether or not the task your group is doing is good for the person you are serving, and to respond quickly and spontaneously to unexpected situations or events. Your print-culture skills would allow you to set goals, stay on task, strategize about the most effective ways to achieve equal justice, and develop new approaches to problem solving.

Neither style of communication is better. One is a natural human way to relate and communicate. The other is a learned style of communicating and relating. Many people facing the crisis of poverty do not have the luxury of reading for their primary information. They are in the "war zone" of poverty. The context of poverty reinforces the need to communicate in a more instantaneous, word-of-mouth, oral-culture style. If the attorney is communicating in a more print-culture style, she or he may be perceived as not caring or not connecting. The oral-culture communicator will see this as rejection and distance. Attorneys can shift this communication breakdown in three ways:

1. Share something about yourself that helps the client see you are just a person.

2. Put the person first, before paperwork or other distractions.

3. Notice and comment on something you have in common with your clients. Humans are way more alike than different. You can share feelings (I am feeling overwhelmed, excited, etc.) or something that goes beyond the task at hand and your role as attorney. Establishing identification with clients is essential to breaking poverty barriers.

A BALANCED LEGAL APPROACH

Exercise: Think of three legal situations where you would use a balance of both the characteristics of orality (spontaneity, comfort with emotion, ability to see our connections to each other and to nature, etc.) and the skills of print culture (organization, analysis, planning ahead, focus, etc.). Write about how you use each characteristic to better serve your clients.

MEANINGS ARE IN PEOPLE, NOT WORDS

Communication theory says meanings are in people, not words. We make meaning from our lived experience. If you add in the different context of poverty, the chances of misunderstanding increase even more.

When I was 15 years old, I told a teacher, "I'm quitting school. This stuff has nothing to do with me." The teacher said, "You need to stay in school because, one day, you will want a job." When thinking about communication theory, what does a "job" mean to a teacher? What does a "job" mean to a migrant labor worker from generations of poverty? The teacher thought she was giving me an incentive to stay in school. From her perspective, a job meant security. It meant a roof over her head, food in her fridge, and her transportation and health needs would be met. A job meant social honor and respect from her fellow human beings.

Conversely, I had watched people work hard my entire life. I never saw any of my illiterate family members "move up" in their jobs. I never saw anyone earn enough to pay both rent and utilities. The only thing jobs did was take me away from my family. We still got evicted, still went hungry, and our cars were still towed because we had no insurance. In poverty, your family needs you to be there because everyone is in crisis. I looked at the teacher and said, "I do not want a job." The teacher responded with, "You are lazy and unmotivated! You are not going to go anywhere in life with that little attitude."

Language and meanings are two different things. Meanings are not in the words that we use, but in the people with whom we communicate. The French have a saying, "Half of what I say belongs to me. The other half belongs to your interpretation of what I say." We use verbal language and other kinds of symbols to try to help others understand the meanings that are in us.

Do not think of words as having absolute meanings? Be sure you have enough interaction in your communication that you have confidence those in the conversation are sharing the meaning rather than just the language. Most of the meaning of words is in the tone of voice, body posture, context, and facial expressions.

delete

Verbal communication is complex. The message that you send verbally and nonverbally may not be the message that is received. To improve communication, practice this: Say it, say it again, say it another way, then ask people what they heard you say. Only when they can repeat it back to you do you know you have created shared meaning.

YOU CANNOT <u>NOT</u> COMMUNICATE

You cannot not communicate. This means that even if you are not speaking or writing, you are sending messages nonverbally to those around you. These nonverbal messages are always being sent. It is important to increase your skills in observing nonverbal behavior, while not being too sure that you're a perfect reader of body language.

> **Example**: The way you sit may tell others that you are tired or alert. Your facial expressions may tell others that you are angry or happy. Someone may look at you and you may interpret it to mean that that person is looking for trouble, when in fact she or he just had something in her or his eye. Your tone of voice may convey messages you did not mean to send. Nonverbal messages are not easy to interpret. What you see or hear may or may not be true. When appropriate, it is always best to clarify in a nonjudgmental and nonthreatening way to get clarification of possible meanings being sent nonverbally.

> **Example**: A woman was preparing to talk to a group of teen moms and dads who were working on their GED's (high school diplomas). After her talk with them, she was going to teach a course at a university. She wanted to be dressed appropriately for both situations, but wouldn't have time to change. She decided to dress for the university event. When she arrived at the GED school, the students looked at her with disappointed looks. Their nonverbals conveyed that they did not feel that someone "like" her could help them. They judged her by her clothing. She was obviously rich and well-educated. They decided that she couldn't possibly know what it was like to be in poverty, uneducated, and

struggling. What they didn't know until she began to speak was that she had grown up in poverty. She had dealt with hunger, homelessness, violence, crime, dropping out of school, and other issues of poverty. After hearing her story, the group began to listen and pay closer attention. They found her insights about how she had made it out of poverty and gotten educated to be valuable and helpful. This is a true story. It is an example of how nonverbals can be a barrier to communication. The students didn't even want to hear the teacher based on the way she was dressed. She was communicating without speaking. Even when we are not speaking or writing, we are communicating through our nonverbal behavior.

NONVERBAL COMMUNICATION

Exercise: Write two or more paragraphs about times that you felt people failed to understand you because they were misunderstanding your nonverbal behaviors. When you write your paragraphs, consider what meaning you think they were giving to what behavior. Why was it wrong? How did it feel? What did you do about it?

www.combarriers.com

Effective Communicating Across Poverty Strategies

Communication
Across Barriers

- Build common ground to increase trust

- Build relationships by sharing something about yourself

- Use multiple approaches until you are assured of shared meaning

- Repeat information that is new

- Break information down into small, doable steps

- Put information in a story about someone like the person you are serving

- Follow up—poverty is constant crisis

Communication
Across Barriers

10 STRATEGIES TO JUMP-START IMPROVED COMMUNICATION

1. Be aware of your own bias, including internal feelings of discomfort around differences. With this awareness, you are more empowered to suspend judgment and share information to help clients succeed in the legal system.

2. Increase follow-through by self-disclosing something about yourself and allowing the client to see you as a real person whom she or he can identify with. Personal connection will go a long way toward showing your client that you are a real human being who cares about her or him.

3. Ensure the messages you send are the messages being heard by paraphrasing, restating with a variety of different examples, asking clarifying questions, and asking the client what she or he heard you say.

4. Be aware of the importance of welcoming facial expressions and positive body language to support your verbal communication.

5. Use visuals as much as possible to accommodate oral-culture communication styles (including drawing out next steps, using bullet points and graphs in written instructions, and using stories as a way to communicate information).

6. Do not expect people to know what may be obvious to you. Use your expertise to coach and navigate people through the legal process.

7. Use active listening techniques, such as suspending your thoughts about what you are going to say in response to the client. Avoid focusing on non-related subjects. Repeat back every so often what you hear to make sure you are understanding correctly and understanding the other person's perspective, explanations, and rationale.

8. There are many lived experiences of poverty. One solution will not work for everyone. Obtain enough information from the client about her or his circumstances to customize your services and be flexible in response to the client's choices of desired next steps.

9. Promote two-way communication (not just what you think would work for clients, but what they think would work best for themselves).

10. Ask open-ended questions to understand clients' perspectives and try to stay away from questions that ask "why," because they can put people on the defense. Instead, use statements such as, "Help me understand" or "Tell me a little more about..."

CASE STUDY!

IMPROVING COMMUNICATION WITH CHAD—LEADING TO EQUAL JUSTICE

Now that you've spent a bit of time with Chad and gotten to know him, you think back on your interactions with him. Are there ways you could have improved the communication with him to better provide legal services?

You remember that Chad was a "no-show" for your first scheduled appointment and that he called several days after the missed appointment to reschedule. He was clearly stressed. If you had had a few minutes, this might have been a good time to take a deep breath, set aside your legal paperwork and thoughts, and just ask Chad how he was doing. It would have been really good to listen carefully to his story and find the points of identification around which you could have built a relationship with him.

A conversation like this in your initial meetings could have helped you to understand his circumstances and realize how what he was going through would impact his ability to follow through with your requests. Knowing about his cancer, you may have thought differently about his shaved head, gaunt face, loose-fitting clothing, and smell of marijuana. This prior knowledge could have assisted you in suspending judgment and working together with Chad to remove obstacles to legal success.

Building that connection during your first two appointments would have allowed you to have a good handle on how to best serve him. You would understand Chad's limited literacy skills and have already assisted (or secured assistance for) him to fill out his client intake form before leaving your office. Because you were aware of the amount of stress in his life and lack of social network, you would have realized the need for supports to assist Chad in obtaining all the required paperwork and background documents that are required to support his case.

Taking the time to understand Chad's situation helps you to become fully prepared to represent him in the courtroom. Building relationships also promotes the type of trust that is needed for Chad to share pertinent information to the case.

Discussion/Reflection Questions

1. How could you make Chad feel welcome and build identification with him in order to better serve his legal needs?

2. Name some ways you could modify your communication style to interact in ways that build trust and assist you in gaining the information you need to provide legal services.

3. How can you have a more balanced communication style when working with clients from poverty situations?

4. What words or examples can you use to motivate your clients? (Remember that meanings are in people, not words.)

Five Keys to Better Serve Your Clients

MODULE 5

FIVE KEYS TO BETTER SERVE YOUR CLIENTS: SUGGESTIONS FOR LEGAL PROFESSIONALS AND COURTS

Learning Objectives:

- Name five key concepts for legal professionals and courts to better serve people living in poverty.

- Explain how focusing on the strengths of clients in poverty can assist you in improving legal outcomes.

- Share the importance of knowing your client's first name and what they see as important.

- Identify potential reasons why a person living in poverty might not follow through with your instructions.

- Learn how attributing motives and judging your clients' behavior can derail legal outcomes.

- Describe strategies for increasing your clients' capacities to successfully complete actions necessary for legal success.

Video Length: 14 Minutes

Below are five easy-to-use practices that will improve communication and relationships across poverty barriers. These concepts are based in theory and provide practical, concrete tools that you can use right away. These strategies, in combination with the best practices in the Breaking Poverty Barriers to Equal Justice video training, provide you with the essential tools for breaking barriers.

Five Keys To Better Serve Your Clients

1. Take a **Strengths Perspective** approach when interacting with your clients.

<u>Strategies</u>:

a. Whenever possible, compliment people on what they have done "right."

b. Empathize with the obstacles they face daily and stand in awe that they are able to keep going.

TAKE A STRENGTHS PERSPECTIVE APPROACH

Every individual has strengths. If you look for problems or what is "wrong" with people, that is what you will see. Have you ever gotten a car that was new to you? Before you got that car, how many did you see on the road? After it was your car, how many did you see? They were everywhere, right?! That is how powerful our perceptive filters are. If you look for what is good about your clients facing poverty, what they do know, and what they have to offer, you will see more legal options.

Five Keys To Better Serve Your Clients

Communication
Across Barriers

2. **Resiliency Theory** says when you treat people as special and value them, you build trust and the capacity for people to grow.

Strategies:

a. Notice people immediately and make them feel valued.

b. Be highly aware of your nonverbals when you talk or meet with your client. Your tone of voice, facial expressions, and body posture will set the tone for your interactions.

Communication
Across Barriers

APPLY RESILIENCY THEORY

Resiliency theory says when you treat people as special, unique individuals and let them know you are happy to be working with them, it builds trust and reduces fear. Talking to an attorney is intimidating. Smiling, making eye contact, and putting a friendly hand on the shoulder can make people feel like you believe in them and are tuned in to their issues. They will likely open up a little more, and that can help you increase their access to receiving justice.

**Five Keys To Better
Serve Your Clients**

www.combarriers.com

Communication
Across Barriers

3. Asset Theory: Everyone has strengths. People in survival mode know a lot. Focus on what they do know and how their skills can be beneficial to their success in the legal system.

Strategies:

a. Listen to narratives of your client's description of the situation. Focus on the internal/external capacities embedded in your client's stories.

b. Also listen to asset gaps clients are experiencing so you can increase their supports and offer solutions that resonate with them.

Communication
Across Barriers

USE ASSET THEORY

Being aware of the internal and external capacities of your clients can assist you in developing solutions that resonate. Internal capacities include resourcefulness, creativity, determination, optimism, mechanical inclination, generosity, etc. External capacities include having a loving/loyal/caring family, money, transportation, housing, childcare, etc. The more you know your clients' capacities, the more empowered you will be to communicate, relate, and build the assets they need to succeed.

Five Keys To Better Serve Your Clients

Communication
Across Barriers

4. Avoid **Faulty Attribution Theory**: attributing motive to others' behavior.

Strategies:

a. Work to develop a foundational understanding of poverty so you will have empathy for the reasons behind your client's behavior.

b. When you feel yourself judging, reflect on the situation and ask yourself if you are expecting your client to do/respond as you would.

Communication
Across Barriers

AVOID FAULTY ATTRIBUTION THEORY

People who do not have a foundational understanding of poverty often guess at the motives behind the behavior of those living in it (e.g., they did not fill out their paperwork because they do not really want their kids back, they were late because they are lazy, etc.). Attributing motives to someone's behavior without seeking to know the why behind the behavior is called faulty attribution theory. These assumptions and value judgments can cause communication and relationship breakdowns and hamper your ability to serve.

Five Keys To Better Serve Your Clients

www.combarriers.com

Communication
Across Barriers

5. Help build **Social Capital** and networks of support. The isolation of poverty perpetuates it.

Strategies:

a. Navigate people to resources and opportunities that will help them to access supports for breaking poverty barriers.

b. Use your title to help people obtain the tools, resources, and knowledge they need to succeed in the legal system.

Communication
Across Barriers

UNDERSTAND SOCIAL CAPITAL THEORY

Practice "community justice." Know your community. Where can a person in poverty go for assistance or opportunities to break barriers to equal justice? Help build social capital and networks of support for breaking poverty barriers. The isolation of poverty perpetuates it. People facing poverty generally only have meaningful connections with others in similar situations. Introduce people to others who can provide a resource or opportunity for moving forward.

What are the conditions and limitations for getting assistance? Are there mentors who might help? Build address books and foster relationships to resources and opportunities.

THE ROLE OF MENTORING IN BREAKING POVERTY BARRIERS

The isolation of poverty perpetuates it and prevents people from succeeding in the justice system. People not only struggle to access equal justice; they have difficulties navigating resources and opportunities for moving out and staying out of poverty. There are specific research-based strategies legal professionals can employ to build the kind of connections necessary for equal access to justice.

In *Beating the Odds: How the Poor Get to College*, Levine and Nidiffer (1996) examined how people from poverty made it to college. This research showed that each participant, regardless of race, attributed his or her success to a mentor who strongly valued and advocated education as a way out of poverty. My research on generational poverty also found that those who made it out of poverty had mentors with very specific qualities (Beegle, 2000).

In this module, I reveal the research-based characteristics needed to mentor and navigate success for people living in the crisis of poverty. Practice these skills in all interactions to break poverty barriers. You do not need to commit to a formal mentoring program to have a profound impact.

FOUR CHARACTERISTICS OF A SUCCESSFUL MENTOR

1. Believe in your clients.

- Most people living in poverty cannot name one person who is making it who believes that they can make it. Those who experience successful outcomes overwhelmingly describe someone who knew the system and who believed they could be successful. State directly that you believe in your clients.

- If individuals struggle to understand what to do next, help them to break it down into doable, manageable steps. Provide encouragement and community partner supports to ensure they have the capacity to follow through and succeed.

2. Believe everyone has knowledge and skills.

- Treat clients like they are knowledgeable and help them realize that they have skills and knowledge to contribute to successful legal outcomes.

- Discover prior knowledge or similar experiences and link your information to that knowledge.

- Use examples and vocabulary that are familiar to those you serve to ensure shared meaning.

3. Have poverty competencies.

- Successful mentoring and navigating will not happen if you are judging your clients. People do not take information from those who are judgmental. You can learn to suspend judgment of clients living in poverty by learning the facts about poverty in your community (for example, how many people get their water shut off every day; the amount of money one adult and two children may receive in cash and food stamps; how much rent is for a modest two-bedroom apartment; who will hire or rent to someone with a felony; how long is the wait list for housing assistance; how many food boxes are given out in one week; etc.). These facts will build your empathy and allow you to incorporate into your examples and requests the realities they face.

- Read about the history of poverty in the U.S. Learn about poverty impacts on equal justice. Explore how we arrived at our current ideas about poverty and the people who live in it. Herbert Gans's (1995) book, The War Against the Poor, is a great one to start with. What are the labels, laws, and policies we have used to address poverty? Learn about President Lyndon Johnson's "War on Poverty." Study models being used to address poverty. The dominant model being used today is the Eligibility Model; it has been shown to be ineffective for breaking poverty barriers, but it is currently used in most federal and state legal programs that serve people in poverty.

- Visit welfare offices, county health or dental clinics, clothing closets, food banks, and other places where people go for assistance in poverty crisis. It will build your understanding of your clients and what they face daily.

4. Reduce isolation: Build your resource backpack.

- As a legal professional, you will not be able to address all of the complexities of poverty that your clients face. Make a point of building your resource backpack. Learn who in your community provides resources and opportunities to people living in poverty. People who are successful in breaking barriers make the time to build a network and link clients to resources and opportunities for breaking barriers.

People from generational poverty who were able to move out and stay out of poverty consistently identified these four mentoring and navigating techniques as critical for breaking the poverty barriers that they faced. Their mentors were from all fields, including education, social service, healthcare, justice, business, and faith-based organizations.

LEVELS OF MENTORING

Mentoring and navigating people to success does not have to be overwhelming. When you take the time to interact in a meaningful way with people living in poverty, you build trust, confidence, and self-esteem, and increase their possibilities. The knowledge that you share cannot be stolen, auctioned, or pawned. You are making a difference.

Communication Across Barriers researchers identified four levels of mentoring that increase success for breaking poverty barriers. Read the descriptions of each level. Think about your own clients and identify strategies you can use to break barriers to equal justice.

To have the most impact, strive to reach the highest level when mentoring.

- **Impacting Comments:** These do not require a long-term commitment or even a dedicated relationship between two people. Here, a truthful passing compliment can lead a person to take a certain path.

- **One-Way Mentoring Relationships:** Many people tell stories of someone who had a tremendous impact on their life. They talk about how the individual consistently treated them in a specific (nurturing) way and all the little things that changed their lives. These relationships are often time-specific.

- **Two-Way Mentoring Relationships:** These relationships can be time-specific or long-term. The main difference between the one-way and the two-way relationship is that the person in the latter knows about the impact s/he is having and continually gets feedback from the person being mentored.

- **Relay Mentoring Relationships:** This relationship starts between two people, with the mentor assisting in whatever way is most appropriate. When other barriers get in the way, the mentor connects the mentee to other mentors who can offer specific assistance or support.

LEGAL BEEGLE ACTIVITY

Legal Beegle

Mentoring and Navigating
Make a Difference

Think back to the person or people who influenced you while you were growing up (a teacher, neighbor, tutor, or friend). Who had the most positive impact on you? Who was your hero? Whom did you look up to? Who navigated you to your legal career? Reflect and write about how this person (or people) helped get you to where you are in life today.

Additional Reflection Questions

Legal Beegle

What did that person do to affect your thinking and actions? What characteristics did he/she have?

Does this person know what kind of impact she/he had on you?

Did you ever express your appreciation for her/his guidance? Why or why not?

Think about a mentor or someone who navigated you through a system you were not familiar with. What did that person do that assisted you in your success with that system? How can you apply those techniques to your clients who most often do not have knowledge of the legal system and their rights?

To gain better knowledge of your community and the resources that might impact your clients, think about clients from different poverty experiences who might be able to assist you in navigating poverty resources and better understanding their circumstances.

As a legal professional working to increase access to equal justice, you may not always know the long-term impact you had, but that in no way lessens its power.

10 PRACTICAL THINGS LAWYERS CAN DO TO INCREASE ACCESS TO JUSTICE

1. Be diligent about looking for cues of bias, including internal feelings of discomfort around differences. With this awareness, we are more empowered to make choices consistent with our values, including equal justice for all.

2. Be aware of the importance of your body language and nonverbal communication to support your verbal communication as you welcome the client and start to get to know him or her.

3. Start to establish trust by building identification with your client. Share some personal information with him or her and look for ways in which you are similar. Do you both have a pet dog? Do you both enjoy a certain sport? That personal connection will go a long way toward showing your client that you are a real human being who cares about him or her and a fair result (especially if you are providing services for free).

4. No one ever makes a decision he or she thinks is stupid. ~~moves forward w/ a decision they think is stupid.~~ By understanding that different life circumstances reward different decisions, we can consciously sidestep judgments and better see the common humanity in the other.

5. Ensure you are understanding your client despite differences between how you and he may organize information. For example, when determining the facts of the case, you might first put your pen down and ask him to tell you what happened. (This also supports the establishment of trust.) Next, ask him to repeat the story and let him know that this time you'll be taking notes. Finally, repeat back the story to see if you have understood. Chances are, even if you took down correctly everything the client said, you will find out more critical information in this third rendition.

6. Ask open-ended questions and try to stay away from questions that ask "why," which can put people on the defense. Instead, use statements such as, "Help me understand," or "Tell me a little more about..."

7. Use common active listening techniques such as repeating back every so often what you hear to make sure you are understanding it correctly and putting yourself in your client's shoes.

8. Ensure your client understands you by accommodating her or his oral-culture communication style. Use visuals as much as possible (including drawing out next steps); make sure your body language supports your verbal communication; use bullet points and graphs in written instructions; use stories as a way to communicate information ("Here is what worked for my client Julie"); summarize every so often; use different examples to convey difficult points, etc. Note that oral culture does not mean that a person cannot read; it means that she prefers information through verbal rather than print means.

9. To minimize the chance of losing your client by inadvertently speaking in legalese, say something like, "I'm used to being around lawyers all day and can sometimes forget how to talk in regular language. If I slip up and use words you're not sure about, please let me know." (This phrasing owns our responsibility as the professional to be clear, rather than asking clients to let us know if "they don't understand.") Use familiar words and examples that laypeople can relate to.

10. One solution does not fit everyone. Obtain enough information from the client to customize your services. And be open to the possibility that, once she has heard your assessment of the case, she may not want to pursue it. If it's going to take five months to get the security deposit back, the case may take a lower priority in her life given other crises going on. Give her a chance to tell you what she wants and recognize that it may be hard for her to express disagreement with you given what she may feel is a large difference in power.

FINAL COMMENTS: GOING BEYOND

Going Beyond

www.combarriers.com

Communication
Across Barriers

- Gain a deeper understanding of poverty: Make an effort to learn the facts about poverty and what people face.

- Go out of your way to listen to the perspectives of people facing poverty to gain insights for meeting people where they are.

- Take a community-wide, poverty-informed approach. Build a full "resource backpack."

Communication
Across Barriers

GOING ABOVE AND BEYOND: SUPPORTING DEEPER CHANGE

- **Gain a Deeper Understanding of Poverty:** Make an effort to learn the facts about poverty in your community and in America. Go out of your way to listen to the perspectives of people facing poverty and hear their narratives to better understand where they are coming from. Read the latest research-based strategies for what works to increase access to justice. Your understanding of poverty and support with legal services can change lives.

- **Be Fearless, Persistent, and Consistent:** Operate like NASA: Failure Is Not an Option. If you cannot connect people to resources or resolve a poverty barrier to equal justice, who in your network or community could? Use an "If not me, then who?" approach when providing legal services.

- **Collaborate and Strengthen Partnerships:** Poverty is complex and requires a comprehensive, community-wide approach. Connect with people, businesses, and organizations outside of the legal profession who can address non-legal barriers. Having a full "resource backpack" (an inventory of community resources for breaking poverty barriers) allows you to focus on the legal aspects that you can assist with. If one does not exist, work to see that one is developed for your community.

LEGAL BEEGLE ACTIVITY

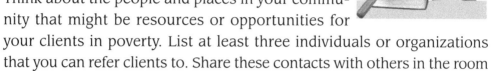

Legal Beegle

Resource Backpack

Think about the people and places in your community that might be resources or opportunities for your clients in poverty. List at least three individuals or organizations that you can refer clients to. Share these contacts with others in the room and with your coworkers.

www.combarriers.com

**Possibilities:
Jennifer Goes to France...Twice**

Communication
Across Barriers

Communication
Across Barriers

With helping professionals reaching out, Jennifer reached more potential at age 17 than most people living in poverty will reach in a lifetime. People made the difference. People going above and beyond their job descriptions to provide access to resources and opportunities changed my life and changed the lives of so many of the next generation. Interrupting generational poverty requires not only reaching out—to the children in poverty, but taking a whole-family approach in working to break the barriers.

Conclusion

Too many people feel like the justice system is the "Titanic" and cannot be turned around. People make up the systems. As an attorney, you have skills and talents that can make a difference for people facing poverty. Thank you for being willing to learn more about poverty and to gain tools for overcoming the barriers poverty imposes. Your services are an essential part of any effort to battle poverty and create a justice system that works for all.

CASE STUDY!

KEYS TO BETTER SERVE YOUR CLIENTS—WHAT YOU CAN LEARN FROM CHAD AND CAROL'S STORIES

Before you were able to take Chad's case to court—Chad was hospitalized again. This time he was told he only had hours to live. His 14-year-old son, Mark, sat by his side—choking back tears and clutching his dad's arm. Chad's family arrived. Chad's sister called Whitney's mother and begged her to let Chad see his daughter before he died. Jamie did not believe her, so she showed up at the hospital alone to see if his sister was telling the truth. When she saw Chad hooked up to life support and on oxygen, Jamie choked up. She left and returned with Whitney. This was the first time Chad had seen Whitney in the past two years, since Jamie had only allowed phone conversations. Chad held onto Whitney and told her how proud he was of her and bragged about what a beautiful girl she had become. Whitney gave her dad a photo and told him how much she loved and missed her daddy. Chad smiled the entire visit. Whitney was allowed to stay for 30 minutes before Jamie said it was time to go. After Whitney left, relatives came back in. Chad proudly showed Whitney's picture to everyone. "Look at my girl. Isn't she beautiful?" Two hours after Whitney's visit, surrounded by his family, Chad took his last breath. He was still clutching Whitney's photo and his son's hand. Chad was only 42 years old.

Like Chad's story, Carol's story is a difficult one, but one with a very different ending. Carol grew up in a middle-class home. She was literate and had a family support system. Carol learned that she had stage-4 metastatic colon cancer. When her husband found out about her cancer, he left her. Her family helped her to get an attorney and the court ordered her husband to pay support. He paid for two months and stopped. She had had a small business but eventually lost it due to a combination of her illness and the bad economy. She had virtually no income and the bank began to foreclose on her home—all while she was fighting for her life. Carol went to legal aid and immediately got assigned to an attorney. A supervising attorney took Carol's ex-husband to court and got him to pay the maintenance he owed, so she didn't have to worry about how to pay for her life while she was fighting desperately to save it. With the maintenance money, Carol was able to catch up on her mortgage, pay her other bills, and remain in her home. With all this support, Carol has been a cancer survivor for 10 years.

Discussion/Reflection Questions

1. Now that you are armed with poverty competencies, how could you have better served Chad and Whitney had you been his attorney from his first attempts to get legal aid?

2. If you were assisting Chad in gaining access to equal justice, how might you assist him? What could have been done to assist Chad in accessing legal services?

3. In addition to providing legal services, what might you do to alleviate the impacts of poverty Chad is facing?

4. Do you see additional points in Chad's experience where he could have benefited from legal advice—outside the custody/visitation scenario?

5. What additional steps could you have taken, as Chad's attorney, to improve his legal outcomes?

6. What was different about the poverty that Chad and Carol experienced? How did these life experiences impact their outcomes?

7. How did Chad's and Carol's life experiences impact their access to legal services?

8. What might have happened if Chad had been so fortunate to have legal representation from the beginning of his struggles?

APPENDIX A

ANSWER KEYS
FOR LEGAL BEEGLE ACTIVITIES

Answers to Test Your Knowledge
of the Impacts of Poverty on Legal Services

Legal Beegle

1. *True.* 2009 data show that we are turning away half of those who need legal services.

2. *False.* Only a small fraction of the legal problems experienced by low-income people (less than one in five) are addressed with the assistance of either a private attorney (pro bono or paid) or a legal aid lawyer.

3. *False.* Only families with annual incomes of 125 percent of the poverty line or less (at or below $29,813 in 2014; $14,588 for individuals) are served. See more at: www.lsc.gov/about/what-is-lsc#sthash.pLYLUWvy.dpuf

4. *True.* Nationally, only one legal aid attorney is available for every 6,415 low-income people. By comparison, there is one private attorney providing personal legal services (those meeting the legal needs of individuals and families) for every 429 people in the general population who are above the LSC poverty threshold.

5. *True.* New data indicate that state courts and specialized courts—especially those courts that handle issues common to people in poverty such as housing and family law—are facing significantly increased numbers of unrepresented litigants.

6. *False.* A growing body of research indicates that outcomes for unrepresented litigants are often less favorable than those for represented litigants.

7. *False.* The difference between the level of legal assistance available and the level that is necessary to meet the needs of low-income Americans is the "justice gap." This includes the civil legal problems of low-income people involving essential human needs, such as protection from abusive relationships, safe and habitable housing, access to necessary health care, disability payments to help lead

Answers to Test Your Knowledge
of the Impacts of Poverty on Legal Services

independent lives, family law issues including child support and custody actions, and relief from financial exploitation.

8. ***True.*** A 2009 study confirmed that the conclusion of the 2005 Justice Gap Report remains valid: There continues to be a major gap between the civil legal needs of low-income people and the legal help that they receive. Legal aid clients are the least likely to receive equal justice.

9. ***False.*** Three out of four clients are women—many of whom are struggling to keep their children safe and their families together.

10. ***False.*** A District of Columbia legal needs study reported that 98 percent of both petitioners and respondents in the Domestic Violence Unit of the D.C. Superior Court were unrepresented; approximately 77 percent of plaintiffs in family court were unrepresented; more than 98 percent of respondents in paternity and child support cases were unrepresented; and 97 percent of respondents in fair housing and eviction court cases were unrepresented.

So, let's summarize:

The vast majority of Americans in poverty receive no legal assistance, even with issues affecting the fundamental rights (allegedly) granted all Americans. Women in poverty bear a disproportionate impact of the lack of legal assistance—and this also disproportionately impacts children. A strong argument could be made that this justice gap is contributing to the ever-widening gap in wealth between the haves and the have-nots in our communities.

Help close the justice gap.
Gain poverty competency skills and
serve people living
in the crisis of poverty.

Answers to Test Your Knowledge
of the Impacts of Poverty on Legal Services

Sources:

- www.lsc.gov/sites/default/files/LSC/pdfs/documenting_the_justice_ga p_in_america_2009.pdf
- The American Bar Association (2009)
- 2012 U.S. Census
- The National Center for State Courts: reports from state and federal courts, as well as individual reports from several states

Legal Beegle

Answers to
Test Your Knowledge...of Poverty in America

Legal Beegle

1. **False.** Inequality of income has gotten worse in the past 25 years. In 2013, the median wealth of the nation's upper-income families ($639,400) was nearly seven times the median wealth of middle-income families ($96,500), the widest wealth gap seen in 30 years when the Federal Reserve began collecting these data. In addition, America's upper-income families have a median net worth that is nearly 70 times that of the country's lower-income families, also the widest wealth gap between these families in 30 years. (Fry and Kocher, PEW Research Center, December 17, 2014.)

2. **True.** The majority of Americans have never had a course on the history of poverty in the United States. Overwhelmingly, what people do know about poverty are stereotypes learned from the media. Students are not taught the structural causes of poverty, such as: unaffordable housing; jobs that do not pay enough to pay rent and utilities and buy food (according to the 2012 report by Bureau of Labor Statistics, 10.6 million individuals were among the "working poor"); lack of access to health and dental care (48 million Americans cannot go to the doctor—even more are without access to dental care); fragmented, underfunded, and often punitive social service systems; underfunded education systems; and lack of public transportation systems to get people where they need to be when they need to be there. Without education and awareness of history and poverty realities, decisions are made, policies are developed, funding is allocated, and people in poverty are often treated badly, which perpetuates the poverty cycle.

3. **True.** In one tiny town in Georgia, a person earning minimum wage can afford a modest two-bedroom apartment, but this is FALSE in the rest of America. The Department of Housing and Urban Development reports that with the exception of the tiny Georgia town, a person earning minimum wage allocates the bulk of his or her income to shelter and has few or no remaining resources for food, electricity, health care, and other basic needs.

Answers to
Test Your Knowledge...of Poverty in America

4. **False.** According to the 2015 Census report, 45.3 million Americans live in poverty. Poverty is defined for a family of four as earning an income below $24,250. We arrive at that income based on the Federal Poverty Guidelines. These Federal Poverty Guidelines are calculated using a formula developed for the cost of living in the 1960s. In the 1960s, economists believed that families spent one-third of their income on food. The formula takes the cost of food and multiplies that by three to calculate a family budget. Families in 2015 do not spend one-third of their budget on food. The bulk of a family's income today is spent on shelter. The 1960s formula does not include health care, transportation, or childcare as part of a family budget. The Economic Policy Institute reports that if you were to add health care, childcare, and transportation to the calculation of a family budget, a family of four would need $48,000 just to provide the basics. The 43.3 million people in poverty identified using the 1960s cost-of-living formula would likely double (or possibly triple) if we were to update the formula for the 2015 cost of living.

5. **True.** Because we have a strong belief in America that everyone has the same chance of making it and because people are uneducated about the realities that people in poverty face, poverty causes are attributed to behavior and choices. A child born into homelessness, hunger, and illiteracy is believed to have the same opportunities as a child born into privilege. We do not take into consideration the impact of environment on behavior and choices. People facing the crisis of poverty are not likely to "behave" and respond in the same way as someone without those stressors does. Do you respond the same when you are stressed as when you are not? Behavior and choices stem from our daily life realities and what we are taught to believe is possible. Those with privilege have the luxury of behaving calmly and making real choices about their future. The crisis of poverty does not always allow you to be "good" and plan ahead for your future. Most people in poverty do what they have to do to get basic survival needs met and to help those they love who are also in crisis. It is hard to think about having a future when your family is hungry today.

Answers to
Test Your Knowledge...of Poverty in America

6. **False.** We are nearing the 2.5 million mark for the number of Americans in prison. The majority of people in prison cannot read at the eighth-grade level. If we continue to incarcerate America's poor, we won't have to talk about affordable housing. We will have to talk about economic impact on our society. The average cost of incarcerating one person for one year is $30,000. In many cities and towns throughout America, prisons are the largest employer and the biggest business. One in every 32 Americans has been or is currently incarcerated. We use prison to try to solve many poverty issues (e.g., people go to prison for writing bad checks to pay rent, selling drugs to buy food, stealing to pay for basic needs). Imagine what would happen if we spent $30,000 per person on training, housing, and education—enabling people to earn a living wage?

7. **False.** We have plenty of privileged people who are alcoholics, drug addicts, child abusers, and law breakers. The difference for privileged people is that if they are addicted to drugs or alcohol, they have resources to get rehabilitation and help. For people in poverty who become addicted, the answer to their addiction is generally incarceration. Few communities in the nation have resources allocated to meet the needs of people in poverty who are drug- or alcohol-affected. A privileged person can buy services; a person in poverty, if lucky, gets on a wait list for help or is given inadequate services. For example, the national average rehab program for someone in poverty who is addicted is between five and 30 days. Research shows that, for many drugs, a minimum of six months to one year of rehab services is needed. The person in poverty who receives 30 days' rehab for a meth addiction is highly likely to fall back into that addiction. The societal response is generally to blame or attribute relapse to personality ("That's just the kind of person they are" or "They really didn't want a better life"). Instead, examine the literature on addictions (which is clear) to many drugs, such as meth, where a year of intensive rehab is recommended.

Answers to
Test Your Knowledge...of Poverty in America

8. **False.** Privilege and power provide the luxury of having the time, vo-cabulary, and knowledge of education norms. My mom would say, "I ain't going in there and make a fool out of myself. Those people want to talk about school. I don't know anything about school. There's no point in me going in there." If someone had asked my mom to come in and tell them about me, she would have been there in a heartbeat. I was her pride and joy; she loved me. We tend to use faulty logic when assessing the behavior of people in poverty. For example: If my child had a conference, I would be there. Therefore, I care about my child. If a parent does not come, it must mean he or she does not care.

9. **False.** Nationally, half of all 4-year-olds in poverty are turned away or put on a wait list. This is despite solid, longitudinal research that shows children who attend Head Start are more ready to learn when they arrive at elementary school and more likely than children who did not attend Head Start to complete their education.

10. **False.** People are not getting rich from begging on the streets. Think about it. Many people are destitute and desperate. They may believe with their education and skills that their only hope in this economy is begging or welfare; neither option provides dignity for human beings.

    In addition, we have a policy that does not allow someone who has a criminal record to receive housing assistance. Many land-lords will not rent to someone with a criminal conviction. Where are these people supposed to go? You can say, "I don't care; they should have thought of that before committing a crime," but the reality is, most people who commit crimes will someday get out of jail or prison. If we won't hire them or rent to them, they will be on our streets and forced to resort to committing crimes again in order to live.

    The average welfare check for one adult and two children in 1986 was $408. The average welfare check in 2015 for one adult and two children is $478—only a $70 increase in almost 30 years.

Answers to
Test Your Knowledge...of Poverty in America

The average disability check is $756. If you have additional children while on welfare, the average increase for a new baby is $60 per month. People do not get rich from welfare. Neither welfare nor disability provides enough for a person to pay for rent and meet their basic needs. HUD reports the average rent for a modest two-bedroom apartment in the U.S. is $750.

11. *False.* Paulo Freire, a world poverty expert, said every society teaches its people what it takes to belong. Abraham Maslow, a human development expert, said that for human beings, belonging is almost as important as eating. We have a basic human need to belong. In the U.S., what messages do we send to people showing what they need to belong? If you are a kid in high school, what kind of tennis shoes do you need? If you can't talk about what is on cable television, you can't be part of many conversations and you do not belong. We teach kids today that they need a cell phone to belong! If we frame the behavior in a societal context, it allows us to address its roots, not blame and judge people for behaving in ways that our society has socialized them to behave.

Finally, cigarette smoking is an addiction. We get angry at people in poverty who smoke. But how much does it cost to quit? Is there access to counseling (real access—transportation, someone to reach out to you and help you access the resource)? Nicorette and other stop-smoking products range from $300 to $500 for just three stages. Smoking has been found to calm nerves. Many people in the crisis of poverty (as well as those in privilege) seek ways to calm nerves and are prey to addictive substances like tobacco.

Answers to
Test Your Knowledge...of Poverty in America

12. *True and False.* True if you are skilled or educated. False if you are an uneducated, unskilled laborer. We know that even one year of college increases income. People in poverty are the least likely to receive an education. In America, we believe if you work hard, you move up. The statistics say this is not true without an education or skill. Who works harder, the migrant labor worker or the person in an office cubicle? If the migrant labor worker hurries to finish his or her row, what does he or she get? The migrant labor worker does not move up. Two-thirds of people in poverty are working 1.7 jobs, according to the Census, and they still cannot pay their rent and buy food. Without education or a skill, the average income increase after working for 10 years in the American labor market is $2.

As you age in the labor market, you are less likely to earn a living wage if you do not have education or a skill. People who work in menial, seasonal, or temporary jobs generally use their "bodies" or physical strength to earn a living. Employers need young, physically healthy workers to perform the physically demanding jobs. Many jobs that used to pay a living wage for those who were uneducated or not skilled are not available due to globalization and automation. Even with the knowledge that unskilled, uneducated workers are not likely to earn a living wage, welfare policy does not allow people on welfare to go to school or get training while receiving benefits to meet their basic needs. We push people into minimum-wage jobs, take away childcare and health care benefits, and watch as many plummet into desperate situations of homelessness, sickness, and incarceration. Many often return to welfare in even worse shape.

Legal Beegle

Answers to Interpretation and Active Listening Activity

Legal Beegle

	True	False	Unknown
1. The wealthy Native American woman opened her purse.			X
2. The purse contained money.			X
3. The wealthy Native American woman had opened the door to her car.	X		
4. The middle-class African American man was a thief.			X
5. The poor White parking garage attendant was the man at the car door.			X
6. The middle-class African American man took the contents of the purse.			X
7. There was a man inside the car.			X
8. The middle-class African American man took the money.			X
9. The wealthy Native American woman owned the car.			X
10. The middle-class African American man was a passenger.			X

Reflect on why you believe you chose the answers you did:

APPENDIX B

SAMPLE APPLICATION FOR CLE CREDIT FOR BREAKING POVERTY BARRIERS FOR EQUAL JUSTICE

(Available online at: www.combarriers.com/equaljustice)

APPLYING FOR CLE CREDIT FOR BREAKING POVERTY BARRIERS TO EQUAL JUSTICE

Note to Facilitator

Thank you for your work to increase knowledge of poverty in the legal services community. The more we all know about poverty, the more effective we will be in breaking barriers to equal justice.

Below is a breakdown of the suggested times and subject matters for inclusion into your state's CLE application. This curriculum should meet your state's requirements for elimination of bias credit.

The entire curriculum, including interactive exercises, takes approximately 4.5 hours. We suggest doing the entire curriculum because the more legal professionals know about poverty, the more likely their communication will be effective and they will make a difference for their client or customer from poverty. If you do not want to commit that much time in one sitting, you could break it up into four shorter sessions, as noted below. In any event, while the video alone is 2.25 hours, we would encourage you to not just show the video, but to actively lead participants through the interactive exercise (or some others that you find effective) because interactive exercises tend to result in more effective and lasting learning.

Options for covering the material in four sequential sessions
- Intro (30 minutes), Module 1 (1.0 hour)
- Module 1 and Module 2 (1.5 hours)
- Modules 3 and 4 (1.5 hours)
- Module 5, Afterword, plus group exercise to list 10 specific strategies for improving communication with clients from poverty (1.0 hours)

Options for stand-alone sessions
- Module 1 and Module 2 (1.5 hours)
- Modules 3 and 4 (1.5 hours)

Proposed Wording for Credit Application

This CLE will be ___ hours in duration and will take place from _____ (time) to _____ (time) on _____ (day/date). The course will fulfill the elimination of bias requirement by addressing biases and barriers in the administration of justice as it pertains to those living in poverty. It also will give legal professionals specific tips for how to better serve those in poverty.

The presentation will consist of five modules, each with specific learning goals. The five modules will each include a video segment of Dr. Donna Beegle teaching a live audience of legal professionals, as well as interactive exercises to deepen attendee learning and engagement.

The credentials of Dr. Beegle:

Donna M. Beegle, Ed.D., is an authentic voice that brings unique insights from having grown up in generational poverty in America. Born into a family of migrant workers who were mostly illiterate and married at 15, Dr. Beegle is the only member of her family who has not been incarcerated. By age 26, she earned her GED, and within 10 years she received her doctorate in educational leadership. Dr. Beegle's inspiring story and work have been featured in newspapers around the nation, on local TV, and on national programs on PBS and CNN.

Dr. Beegle shares her life experiences and insights gained from years of studying poverty as she speaks, writes, and trains across the nation to break the iron cage of poverty. For more than 25 years, she has traveled to hundreds of cities, covering 48 states and five countries, to assist professionals with proven strategies for breaking poverty barriers. She has worked with educators, justice professionals, health care providers, social service agencies, and other organizations that want to make a difference for those living in the crisis of poverty. Her clients have included the Washington Municipal Judges Association, Kansas City Supreme Court, the National Association of Court Administrators, and the Oregon Department of Justice. Dr. Beegle has presented for the National Association for Court Management, Oregon Bar Association, Minnesota Bar Association, and North Dakota Bar Association, and for judges in Kansas, Washington, New York, Colorado, Arizona, Michigan,

Florida, Illinois, and Missouri. She has twice conducted trainings for the chief magistrates in Trinidad and Tobago.

She and her organization, Communication Across Barriers, have received numerous awards, including National Speaker of the Year from the New Mexico State Bar Foundation and the Oregon Ethics in Business award, and Dr. Beegle was recently named a Princeton Fellow. In 2010, Portland State University's School of Social Work dedicated the Donna M. Beegle Community Classrooms in her honor.

Dr. Beegle is the author of *See Poverty...Be the Difference* and *An Action Approach to Educating Students in Poverty*.

The credentials of the facilitator:
Insert credentials of person facilitating the training.

Course Content
INTRODUCTION

Video – 3 min
Discussion – 15 min

Key Concept:
• The importance of understanding poverty to provide high-quality legal services to those in poverty.

Exercises/Discussion: Participants will be encouraged to examine their beliefs and assumptions about poverty and its impact on access to the legal system.

Module 1: Understanding Poverty from an Insider's Perspective: Why It's Essential to Breaking Barriers to Equal Justice

Video – 21 min

Discussion – 15 min

Key Concepts:

- Gain insights into how people living in poverty experience the justice system.
- Share why it is important for legal professionals to understand the experiences of those living in the crisis of poverty.
- Understand how vocabulary and different styles of communication can be barriers to accessing the legal system.
- Name where most people get their knowledge of what it's like to live in poverty.
- Identify some specific poverty barriers to obtaining equal justice.
- See why those in poverty may not even seek the assistance of a lawyer, and learn ways to remedy that.
- Know how the isolation of people living in poverty reduces access to justice.
- Describe the importance of legal professionals gaining self-awareness and self-reflection on their beliefs about poverty and those who live in it.

Exercises/Discussion: Participants will be encouraged to examine their beliefs and assumptions about the current state of poverty in the United States. To deepen understanding of the material presented, participants will also be introduced to "Chad," a client in poverty needing legal help, and discuss how to use concepts learned to give Chad the best service possible. (Chad's story will be developed more in each module so participants can gain immediate and practical experience in applying the concepts to real life situations.)

Module 2: Defining Poverty and Understanding Its Impacts on Justice: The Experiences of Those in Poverty in Our Society and in Our Legal System

Video—49 min

Discussion—20 min

Key Concepts:

- Understand how lack of knowledge about poverty and its impacts on people prevents legal professionals from meeting the legal needs of those who live in the crisis of poverty.
- Name some facts about poverty in America, including the current minimum wage in your state.
- Describe how people living in poverty often experience the justice system, including law enforcement, and how that differs from the middle-class experience.
- Describe the financial reality of living in poverty and its impacts on access to legal services.
- Name why working hard is not enough to achieve economic stability, and the two variables that can change that.
- Describe four life experiences called "poverty" and the different impact of each on access to legal services.
- Understand the intersections of race and poverty, and the danger of calling poverty a race issue.

Exercises/Discussion: Participants will be encouraged to reflect on the following questions and discuss their implications for equal justice: Why a person from poverty might be more likely to run from the police and why that might differ from the reaction of someone from the middle class or wealth; how social class experience shapes one's worldview and actions; how those actions might not make sense within the context of another social class.

Module 3: Examining Assumptions About Poverty: How Universal Access to Justice Depends on Legal Professionals Being Able to See and Suspend Judgments of "Others"

Video—14 min

Discussion—15 min

Key Concepts:
- Understand how stereotypes and myths reduce our ability to provide equal justice.
- Learn why it's common to go to blame and judgment when we see the choices of people in poverty.
- Describe specific ways that judging clients in poverty can cripple effective communication.
- Develop awareness of unconscious bias and how bias can lead to decisions about whom we will assist and whom we will not help.
- Gain "active listening" skills including the ability to suspend thoughts or judgments that prevent understanding the perspectives and strengths of your clients.
- Learn why communicating with someone from a different background can cause misunderstandings and leave clients not knowing what to do next.
- Describe root causes of poverty.
- Understand how the need to "belong" drives motivation and choices that are often judged by those not in poverty.

Exercises/Discussion: Participants will examine their own assumptions and the impact of assumptions on their commitment to provide high-quality legal services to any given person. They will experience the impact assumptions can make on their ability to accurately hear a story.

Module 4: Improving Communication Across Poverty Barriers: Overcoming Other Barriers to Equal Justice When Serving People from Poverty

Video—28 min

Discussion—30 min

Key Concepts:

- Name five common reasons why communication between a legal professional and a client in poverty might break down.
- Share three levels of self-disclosure in communication and which level builds trust between legal professionals and clients.
- Describe how to create common ground and build identification to improve communication across poverty barriers.
- Explain how word of mouth (oral culture) styles of communicating and relating differ from literate (print culture) styles of communicating and how the differences can cause misunderstandings.
- Describe the importance of sharing the "why" behind your actions.
- List some specific communication strategies legal professionals can use to communicate more effectively with clients who are more oral culture communicators.

Exercises/Discussion: Participants will be introduced to the power of identification and what it is based on. They will learn when and how print culture can serve them; and when and how oral culture can serve them. They will identify their own dominant style for communicating and how this impacts their clients from poverty in their access to justice. They will be able to name specific strategies for providing legal service and identify whether they stem from print culture or oral culture. Participants will learn the importance of nonverbal communication and impacts when it is not consistent with verbal communication. They will also learn strategies to jump-start improved communication.

Module 5: Five Keys to Better Serve Your Clients: Suggestions for Legal Professionals and Courts

Video—14 min

Discussion—20 min

Key Concepts:

- Name five key concepts for legal professionals and courts to better serve people living in poverty.
- Explain how focusing on the strengths of clients in poverty can assist you in improving legal outcomes.
- Share the importance of knowing your client's first name and what they see as important.
- Identify potential reasons why a person living in poverty might not follow through with your instructions.
- Learn how attributing motives and judging your clients' behavior can derail legal outcomes.
- Describe strategies for increasing your clients' capacities to successfully complete actions necessary for legal success.

Exercises/Discussion: Participants will reflect on the importance of mentors to the success of a person in poverty (and why). They will discuss what characterizes a good mentor and which characteristics of a good mentor an attorney can adopt to become more effective in promoting clients' success. They will learn 10 practical steps they can take to improve access to justice.

Afterword—Going Beyond

Discussion—15 min

Participants will discuss what resources they have at their disposal to help those in poverty navigate an unfamiliar middle-class system and they will share those resources with others in the room (or with whom they work) to compile a list for later use. Participants should revisit the first (introduction) scenario. Other next steps as decided by the group.

APPENDIX C

ATTORNEY-CLIENT CHECKLIST

(Available online at: www.combarriers.com/equaljustice)

ATTORNEY-CLIENT CHECKLIST

Some of what I can give you:

- I am not going to charge you because I believe you deserve to have someone who knows the courts and laws regarding your case. I am committed to making sure that your rights are respected and you get the help you need.

- I can explain the law and your rights. I can help you know what to do. I will also help you understand what can happen if you do not follow the law.

- I will explain several different choices you have right now. I will also explain how they might play out when you enter the legal system so you are fully aware of what you are getting into.

- I will let you know any updates to your case and return your phone calls as soon as I possibly can. I can call you back sooner if you let me know something is urgent.

- As your attorney, I have to keep all of your information confidential. So, you don't need to worry about me repeating negative information. Everything you share with me about your life and situation will be private unless you tell me it is okay to share.

- If I can't help you with something, I will do my best to connect you with someone who will know where you might be able to get help.

- I will try to work around what is going on in your life when making appointments.

- I will sign a written agreement telling you what I will do for you. I will answer any questions you have about our agreement to work together.

- I have a license to practice law in our state and am in good standing with the ethics board.

It will help me represent you better if you:

- Help me understand what is going on in your case. The more you tell me about your situation, the better I can help you. Please share all the facts with me —even things that may not seem important, or things that may make your look bad, or things that you think might upset me. I need to know everything. The other attorney or others involved in the case may find out or share information that you have not told me. It would be better if I know the whole story from you and come up with a plan for how to deal with it before I am surprised by it. If I don't know your full story, the advice I give you might not be what is best for your situation.

- Tell me what you want to happen. If I know your goal for the case, I am better prepared to assist you.

- I will explain what it will take to meet your goals. If that is too much, let me know. Sometimes the legal system can feel like it is more work than it's worth.

- If you do not understand when I explain something, please do not feel bad. Interrupt me and ask me to explain it again or to explain it in another way. Before you see me, think of questions you have for me. If you want to, write them down and bring your list of questions to your appointment. I am happy to answer your questions and make sure we are working together for the best possible outcomes.

- Please tell me the best way to reach you. Let me know other ways to contact you (like a family member and close friend), just in case I can't reach you at your number. I like to have multiple ways of getting in touch with you. My goal is to make sure we are communicating so you get the best legal representation.

- When I contact you, please get back to me as quickly as you can. Legal issues move fast and we will need to be in touch.

- The legal system requires certain paperwork, so I might give you a list of things to gather in order to best represent you. Do not feel bad if you need help getting the paperwork or filling it out. We will try to help or find others who can help you.

- If at all possible, try to arrive about 15 minutes early to our appointments. Then, if I happen to finish early with another person, I might have some extra time to spend with you! If something comes up which will make you late, please let me know as soon as you can. I might have a meeting scheduled right after your appointment, but I want to spend as much time with you as possible. Also, if something comes up and you are unable to make the appointment, let me know this as quickly as you can, so I may meet with others who need legal assistance.

- If other legal issues come up in addition to what we agreed I'd help you with, please let me know. It will not be good if something comes up later in the case that I do not know about. If I know the other legal issues, I may be able to assist or connect you to someone who can help.

- Will you let me know right away if something happens in your case, such as:

_____

_____

_____

_____

ABOUT DR. DONNA M. BEEGLE

Donna M. Beegle, Ed.D., is an authentic voice that brings unique insights from having grown up in generational poverty in America. Born into a family of migrant workers who were mostly illiterate and married at 15, Dr. Beegle is the only member of her family who has not been incarcerated. By age 26, she earned her GED, and within 10 years she received her doctorate in educational leadership. Dr. Beegle's inspiring story and work have been featured in newspapers around the nation, on local TV, and on national programs on PBS and CNN.

Dr. Beegle shares her life experiences and insights gained from years of studying poverty as she speaks, writes, and trains across the nation to break the iron cage of poverty. For more than 25 years, she has traveled to hundreds of cities, covering 48 states and five countries, to assist professionals with proven strategies for breaking poverty barriers. She has worked with educators, justice professionals, health care providers, social service agencies, and other organizations that want to make a difference for those living in the crisis of poverty. Her clients have included the Washington Municipal Judges Association, Kansas City Supreme Court, the National Association of Court Administrators, and the Oregon Department of Justice. Dr. Beegle has presented for the National Association for Court Management, Oregon Bar Association, Minnesota Bar Association, and North Dakota Bar Association, and for judges in Kansas, Washington, New York, Colorado, Arizona, Michigan, Florida, Illinois, and Missouri. She has twice conducted trainings for the chief magistrates in Trinidad and Tobago.

She and her organization, Communication Across Barriers, have received numerous awards, including National Speaker of the Year from the New Mexico State Bar Foundation and the Oregon Ethics in Business award, and Dr. Beegle was recently named a Princeton Fellow. In 2010, Portland State University's School of Social Work dedicated the Donna M. Beegle Community Classrooms in her honor.

Dr. Beegle is the author of *See Poverty...Be the Difference* and *An Action Approach to Educating Students in Poverty*.

RESOURCES

See Poverty...Be The Difference: Discovering the Missing Pieces for Helping People Move Out of Poverty

This resource provides an authentic opportunity for gaining a foundation, rooted in lived experience and research, for understanding poverty and addressing its impacts. It is designed to shatter stereotypes with facts about poverty and to provide concrete tools and ideas for creating programs and systems that are responsive to the needs of people living in poverty conditions. Please use it as a tool to help you be the missing piece and truly make a difference for students and families who live in poverty.

Coming Soon

The Donna Beegle Story

This autobiography tells the story of how Dr. Beegle grew up in generational poverty, dropped out of school at 15 years of age to get married, and was a 25-year-old single mother with two kids when she joined a program that changed her life. This book tells about the experiences and education that helped Dr. Beegle form the processes and strategies to help people move out of and stay out of poverty.

To purchase any additional resources by Dr. Beegle, email books@combarriers.com or visit www.store.combarriers.com

To have Dr. Beegle speak at your organization or provide personalized training to your community, please contact Communication Across Barriers, 503-590-4599, dbeegle@combarriers.com.

Intro ~~acknowledge time~~
Set Appts 3
Acknawledge time
Activity Brainstorm

Insiders Persp.